Data-Driven Instructional Leadership

Rebecca J. Blink, Ph.D.

EYE ON EDUCATION

6 DEPOT WAY WEST, SUITE 106

LARCHMONT, NY 10538

(914) 833–0551

(914) 833–0761 fax

www.eyeoneducation.com

Library of Congress Cataloging-in-Publication Data

Blink, Rebecca J.
Data-driven instructional leadership / by Rebecca J. Blink.
     p. cm.
   ISBN 1-59667-037-1
   1. School management and organization—United States—Data processing. 2. Academic achievement—United States. 3. Educational accountability—United States. I. Title.
LB2806.17.B58 2006
379.1′58—dc22

                                    2006030199

10 9 8 7 6 5 4 3 2

Editorial and production services provided by
Richard H. Adin Freelance Editorial Services
52 Oakwood Blvd., Poughkeepsie, NY 12603-4112
(845-471-3566)

Dedication

This book is dedicated to my parents, Elaine and Earl Blink. Without their support, this book would never have come to fruition. My mom is the best proofreader and editor on the planet! She graciously waded through countless drafts and revisions of this manuscript full of educational jargon and data tables with great care and diligence, all the while providing me with great feedback and encouragement. My parents have always supported my educational efforts—from elementary school through my doctoral work at the University of Wisconsin–Madison. I am, and will always be, eternally grateful for their unyielding commitment to me and my educational journey. Mom and Dad, I hope that after all these years, I have made you proud.

I am certain that the work you see here will make you proud. All of those college credits you paid for are finally getting put to good use. I can't thank you enough for all that you have done for me. I love you very much!

Acknowledgments

First and foremost, I would like to thank Victoria Bernhardt, Ph.D., whose ideas I have incorporated into my work in my own school district. Vickie, you are someone whom I can call a friend and colleague. Thank you so much for your help and for encouraging me to write a book about the Data-Driven Instructional System model and about driving the use of data down to the classroom level, where it can have a positive effect on the instructional process for all children. I will be forever grateful to you for helping me break into the business as an author.

Robert Sickles, president and publisher of Eye On Education, also deserves my thanks. Thank you for your willingness to take a risk on a new, starry-eyed author who thought she might have an idea worth writing about. I was thrilled at the opportunity to harness my ideas and to put them down on paper with the possibility of sharing them with the world.

It would be impossible to go without thanking Scherie Lampe, Ph.D., the university professor who saw my potential before I even knew it existed. Thank you for believing in me more than 20 years ago and making me believe that no matter how difficult it may be to change the organizational structures of some of the most stoic institutions in history, it can be done if there is enough passion in your heart and drive in your stride.

The two school districts that are the cornerstone of this book deserve my appreciation, as they allowed me to conduct teacher and administrative interviews, participate in activities, and observe their hard work in action. Thank you for opening the doors of your buildings and classrooms to me and making me feel welcome. I could not have completed this book without the openness of the teachers and administrators in both districts. You are all fabulous individuals!

Special thanks go to Dr. Richard Halverson, my doctoral advisor at the University of Wisconsin–Madison. Dr. Halverson was able to capture my ideas in graphic form and helped create the visual for the Data-Driven Instructional System (DDIS) Model.

Last but not least, I would like to thank my family and friends, who put up with my long hours of writing, revising, and editing and who knew that this was work that I felt I *had* to complete for myself more than anyone else. Your compassion and understanding is greatly appreciated. I could not have completed this work without you.

Foreword

This book is for you if you believe these two premises about education:

1. All students can learn; and

2. Educators make a difference in the life of every child.

Think back to the time when you were at your first teaching interview and were asked the question, Why do you want to become a teacher? Chances are your answer was: Because I want to make a difference in the lives of children. However, after you accepted that first teaching job, did you begin to get bogged down with the management of all that teachers do? Did you veer away from that dream in order to "cover the curriculum"? Did you put your original goal on hold because you got caught up in all of the managerial things that go along with teaching? If you have since moved into the field of educational administration, does your focus remain on being the type of leader who can make a difference in the lives of children? Reflect on your own practices and beliefs to see if they remain in alignment with your original goal of making a difference in the lives of children. If you feel so overwhelmed with the work that you are now doing that you cannot seem to refocus on why you went into education in the first place, then this book is for you.

Education is a common theme for presidential elections, and the *No Child Left Behind Act of 2001* has added accountability at all levels of the educational process. It is no longer acceptable to simply teach the content of a course. Teachers must make sure that their students comprehend the content of a course so they can meet or exceed accountability standards set up by their state. The question remains: Just how is a school district supposed to ensure that all of its students are mastering the content taught in every course?

Data-Driven Instructional Leadership is a book for every school leader and every teacher. This book provides school districts with a framework for school improvement called the Data-Driven Instructional System (DDIS). It explains the components of the system and gives examples from school districts that are using the DDIS framework to organize their school improvement efforts. The book is written from the practitioner's perspective, so it is very clear how the DDIS model can change the entire organizational structure of a school district. *Data-Driven Instructional Leadership* moves beyond the typical school improvement book and plunges the reader right into the journey of improvement taken by the two districts highlighted in the book. It is written in a conversational style that is easy for everyone to understand

and embrace. This book will help you renew your focus on students and their educational journeys.

Rebecca J. Blink, PhD, makes sharing this message her passion. She has been working in a data-driven system for almost 10 years. Creating a model for districts to follow while implementing a data-driven system developed naturally through her work, *Data-Driven Instructional Leadership* provides the guidance you need as a teacher or school district leader to move your district into the data-driven arena.

Victoria L. Bernhardt
Executive Director
Education for the Future
400 West First Street, Chico, CA 95929-0230
530-898-4482, fax 530-898-4484
vbernhardt@csuchico.edu
http://eff.csuchico.edu

Table of Contents

Introduction

How do educational leaders design a school system that provides the best chance for growth for all students? How do we build a system in which all avenues lead to improvements in student achievement? How do we nurture a culture of continuous improvement while fostering an environment of high expectations and accountability? With the No Child Left Behind (NCLB) Act of 2001 looming over school districts nationwide, school leaders are searching for answers to these questions.

School districts across the country are scrambling to meet the requirements of the NCLB—particularly the requirement that 100% percent of students must earn a proficient or advanced score on their state reading and math tests by the 2013–14 school year. Can any school district ever achieve perfection? Simply by the nature of its enforcement, NCLB requires that all school districts become perfect by 2013–14. There are absolutely some elements of NCLB that I believe are long overdue; however, there are other elements that I believe are unattainable by any school district under the current requirements of the act.

For example, I have a relative, "Paul," who has been identified with a cognitive disability. To look at him and have a conversation with him, you would never know that he has a disability. He can carry on a conversation with anyone using vocabulary that is well above his level of intelligence. Paul is a very social and polite person. He is not withdrawn or shy at all. Although it is not severe, Paul's disability limits his ability to learn and retain information at the same rate as his grade-level peers. His disability was identified during kindergarten, and he is now a sophomore in high school. Paul's teachers have known of his disability for his entire educational career. However, making his teachers aware of his disability and putting a law in place that demands he be proficient in reading and math at a level that is comparable to his grade-level peers are two very different things. Although NCLB requires Paul's district to focus his educational program on academics rather than on life skills, he still does not perform at a level that is acceptable under the law. Paul's doctors say that he may never be able to perform at a level equivalent to that of his grade-level peers. When he does not perform at the proficient level, his school and district could face extreme sanctions under NCLB. Granted, he would have to be one of many special education students not performing at the proficient level for the district to be held accountable, but it could happen. Is it fair to expect him to perform at a level that may not even be medically possible?

I unquestionably agree with the accountability clause of NCLB because I have witnessed firsthand what a difference it has made in the curriculum that Paul is exposed to. Before NCLB, he was wiping off tables in the commons after the other students ate their lunches, mopping floors in the gym after events, and filling the soda machine in the teachers' lounge. Now, he must take classes that may someday help him learn to read. Why wasn't he in those classes throughout his educational career? Why did it take a federal mandate for someone to realize that maybe Paul should be in classes that teach him to read if he is expected to learn to read? Although the law is not perfect, it is a step in the right direction, as I believe—and this is the heart of all public education—that every child deserves an education. Paul is one example of why NCLB is needed. Through no fault of its own, the district in which Paul goes to school did not have an appropriate educational program for him until it was forced to do so under the provisions of NCLB.

However, there are some issues that need to be addressed in order to account for students who simply may not be able to demonstrate proficiency by 2013–14. How is it possible for school districts across the country to have 100% of their students at a proficient or advanced level in reading and math by the year 2013–14? Although there are provisions in the law that allow school districts to have 1%–2% of their special education population assessed using an alternate assessment, all other special education students must take a standardized assessment that meets NCLB requirements for their state. Public education institutions across the nation are being held to higher standards in the 21st century than ever before in the history of schooling. States are requiring students to perform at higher levels, and teachers are being held accountable for the learning of their students rather than simply the delivery of instruction. It is no longer good enough to simply teach a subject, as in Paul's case—it is necessary for students to learn something. Student learning must be documented within the district, or else federal funding could be reduced or eliminated for K–12 school districts that do not demonstrate improvement and meet the requirements of NCLB. Some states have even instituted benchmarks for proficiency levels between now and the 2013–14 school year. Wisconsin is one of those states. Beginning with the 2001–02 school year, the state of Wisconsin instituted periodic benchmark targets for the percentage of students reaching a proficient or advanced level in reading and math. In 2009–10, those increments will increase on a yearly basis until the 2013–14 goal of 100 percent proficiency in reading and math is reached.

Benchmark Percentages for Reading and Math: State Assessment in Wisconsin, 2001–02 to 2013–14

School Year	01–02	02–03	03–04	04–05	05–06	06–07	07–08
Reading	61%	61%	61%	67.5%	67.5%	67.5%	74%
Math	37%	37%	37%	47.5%	47.5%	47.5%	58%

School Year	08–09	09–10	10–11	11–12	12–13	13–14
Reading	74%	74%	80.5%	87%	93.5%	100%
Math	58%	58%	68.5%	79%	89.5%	100%

Let's take a moment to review the legislative and political road that led to the reauthorization of the Elementary and Secondary Education Act (ESEA). What happened that caused all of this attention to be paid to schools and state systems of accountability? The 2000 presidential campaign brought a renewed focus on educational accountability. On January 8, 2002, newly elected President George W. Bush signed into law the reauthorization of the ESEA, commonly referred to as the No Child Left Behind Act. The act, which embodies President Bush's educational reform plan, was sent to Congress on January 23, 2001 and marked the most sweeping reform of the ESEA since its enactment in 1965.

NCLB redefines the federal role in K–12 education and is designed to close the achievement gap between disadvantaged and minority students and their peers. NCLB is based on four basic principles: stronger accountability for results, increased flexibility and local control, expanded options for parents, and an emphasis on teaching methods that have been proven to work (for more information, see http://www.ed.gov). Now, public school districts across the country are trying to comply with the demands of this new legislation. School districts need information, and they need it fast. For the first time in the history of K–12 public education, federal funding will be based on student achievement.

Under the new legislation set forth in NCLB, all students in the third through the eighth grade will be tested in the areas of reading and math (see ESEA, Part A, Subpart 1, Section 1111–[3][2][vii]). If any achievement gaps are identified through the testing process, the school district must address those issues and develop a plan for improvement. In order to identify gaps in achievement, an assessment must be administered that measures how much students have learned, not necessarily how much they have been taught. An assessment that measures what a student has learned is different from an assessment that measures what has been taught. The former measures the learning achieved by the student (mastery of content), whereas the latter measures or tracks what the instructor has taught (content). Something can be taught by an instructor and not necessarily mastered by a student. This new federal legislation forces school districts to meet escalating accountability requirements while continually improving student learning.

Therefore, under the new law, it is possible for a high-achieving school district to meet the accountability requirements of NCLB (a certain percentage of students performing at or above the proficient level in a single measured academic area) while failing to show improvement in its overall scores. For example, a school district could have 98% of students performing at the targeted benchmark for its state in a certain tested academic area but still be identified for improvement because it has students like Paul who are not scoring at the targeted benchmark and fall into one of the measured subgroups: socioeconomically disadvantaged, ethnicity, special educational need, or limited English proficiency. The distinction here is that it is no longer good enough for a school district to simply score well (above the calculated average for the state in the year of administration) in each of the measured academic areas of reading and math. Under the new law, every school district must improve by closing any identified achievement gaps on the state assessments (ESEA, Title I, Section 1001, Statement of Purpose, Parts 1–12), regardless of how the district scores overall.

By the academic school year of 2013–14, the U.S. Department of Education demands that every local school district in the country have 100% of students performing at the two highest levels of the state assessment (advanced or proficient) in reading and math (ESEA, Part A, Subpart 1, Section 1111–[3][F]). In order to meet these accountability demands, NCLB requires that states develop an accountability system to assess and track the progress of all students. Although some severely disabled students will be excluded from the state accountability testing for obvious reasons, a minimum of 95% of students enrolled in a tested grade level must participate in the statewide assessments.

Two subgroups of students may qualify to take an alternate assessment: students with disabilities and students who have limited English proficiency. However, just because a student is a member of one of these subgroups, that does not necessarily mean the identified student will automatically take the alternate assessment. An Individualized Education Plan team meeting must be conducted to determine whether a student is eligible for the alternate assessment for his or her subgroup.

According Angela Pascopella, "Students with disabilities and without severe cognitive disabilities will be expected to reach grade-level standards under the new legislation" (2003, p. 24). In the same article, Bruce Hunter, director of public policy for the American Association of School Boards says,

"There is no way that in the short run, we could avoid having kids with disabilities have a pretty tough time meeting those requirements." Hunter goes on to say, "If you look at standards of proficiency according to the National Assessment of Educational Progress (NAEP), which assesses what students know and can do in certain subjects, those standards are very high. In order for children to read proficiently, they must make inferences about themselves and life. Special education kids are supposed to be moving to proficiency under NCLB. By definition, they have a disability that hinders their education" (24–26). If school districts do not meet these demands from the federal government, funding will be reduced or eliminated and the school and/or district will be labeled a "school identified for improvement."

Preparing school districts for the ramifications of NCLB presents a considerable challenge. The increased attention and focus of legislators at all levels on public education provides the impetus for building and implementing a data-driven instructional system that will ensure improvements in student achievement while closing identified achievement gaps. Don't get me wrong—this is a good thing. Public school districts will be held accountable for the learning of every child in their system. Federal funding for public schools hangs in the balance. If schools do not perform and close the achievement gap identified by their state assessments, they risk not only losing federal funding but also being taken over by federal and state government agencies for "restructuring." American public school systems are scrambling to discover instructional practices that will work for all students.

In the pages of this book, educational leaders will find a framework that will help them organize their school district to become data driven, to identify and close achievement gaps, and to meet the requirements of NCLB. This book will help educational leaders design a data-driven instructional system that will bring their district to the pinnacle of using data to drive classroom instruction. This book will explain the components that need to be in place structurally and give educational leaders suggestions for implementation. This book will teach educational leaders how to orchestrate systemic change in their district to have the most impact on student achievement and to meet the needs of individual students while addressing the accountability requirements of NCLB. How can this be accomplished as a district or building-level administrator? Very consciously and very calculated. Meticulous planning and preparation are the keys to successful implementation.

States and districts have responded to the call for increased accountability by creating links between standards and assessments in schools. Each state in the nation is responsible for responding to the challenge of increased accountability pressures in its own way. School leaders are wrestling with a multitude of issues in their buildings, from assessment to morale, and they are desperately seeking ways to plan for continuous improvement while meeting the needs of all learners, striving to attain the measures of accountability, and respecting the creativity and individuality of the teaching staff. Now more than ever before, school leaders are faced with the need for a comprehensive global plan to inspire the staff in their districts. This book provides that global plan. This book provides the hope that teachers and school districts need, not only to reach and teach their regular education students and move them along the continuum of proficiency but also to address the needs of children like Paul. Students like Paul may never reach the same level as their grade-level peers, but the DDIS model explained in this book will help teachers meet Paul's needs in a way that allows him to demonstrate growth toward the performance of his grade-level peers. Every child deserves an education, and that is what NCLB ensures. This book provides a road map for teachers, administrators, and district-level school officials as they organize a system around students—as it should be.

1

Overview of the Data-Driven Instructional System Model

Making Sense Out of Chaos

As educational leaders, we are relentlessly told that we should use data to drive our instructional decisions. That makes perfect sense to most of us and comes as no big surprise. However, until now, no one has ever explained how to make that happen in a school district when so many ancillary components are bombarding the everyday operations of schools. How to begin to organize such a massive change in a school district and conceptualize the implementation of that change remains the biggest obstacle related to Data-Driven Instructional Systems (DDIS). How and when should the data be gathered, and what data should be included? How does using data to drive instructional decisions affect programming? How does using data to drive instructional decisions affect staffing? How does using data to drive instructional decisions affect what is actually taught at the classroom level? How does a district provide time for teachers and administrators to evaluate and analyze the data they do have? How does using data to drive instructional decisions affect professional learning? How does using data to drive instructional decisions affect goal setting? All of these questions—and more—need to be thought through and planned for before a district can begin to delve into a data-driven initiative. But this task is not as difficult or as overwhelming as it sounds when it is carefully planned and when the implementation is clearly mapped out for all district stakeholders.

In working with educators for almost 20 years—and having been a teacher myself—I have found them to be a very self-effacing group. Teachers do not like to draw attention to themselves, and they do not consider themselves better than anyone else. What happens when an educator from a successful school district is asked to explain exactly what makes his or her students so successful? He or she looks at you with a blank look and tries to explain in what can best be described as organized chaos. Many things coming from all angles in a school system contribute to students' success in the classroom. Typically, there are so many components that make a school district successful that is difficult for those who are successful to describe what they do—or the part they play within the larger system. Often, the most successful educators view their success as simply a product of doing their job. It's what they do every day. These people do not realize how incredibly rare it is to be able to put all of the pieces of the puzzle together in an organized manner while still improving student achievement and meeting the needs of all students. Wouldn't it be helpful to capture the vision of these successful districts, teachers, and school systems and create a model for all school districts to follow? That is exactly what this book does.

I'd like to tell you a story about how I began thinking about this topic and how the model described in this chapter came to fruition. My district, fairly successful and progressive with the latest "cutting-edge" ideas in education, began to attract the attention of school districts across the state. They wondered exactly what was going on in my district that allowed us to be so successful. I have been asked on countless occasions to talk with administrative teams, teacher teams, curriculum councils, full district staffs, and even school board members about why my district has been so successful. Everyone wants to know what we are doing and how we are using data. Here is my story.

As one of those administrators who believed I was just doing my job, whenever I was asked why my district was so successful and what was going on, I would simply answer, "Oh, I don't know that we are doing anything differently than other districts. We work hard and we pay attention to the data that we have on students. We adjust instruction accordingly and hope in the end that we have made a difference. We don't worry about our performance on state assessments because we believe that if we do our jobs well, those assessments will take care of themselves." Well, as I later found out, there is much more to district success than haphazard ideas that simply fall into place. It is no accident that we have been successful. You've all heard the saying that sometimes it is better to be lucky than good. Well, in this instance, you have to be good to be lucky! Designing and implementing a data-driven system that is the catalyst for school improvement must be a very calculated and meticulous process. Without realizing it, I had created such a system in my district—and I believe that school districts across the country can emulate this system in order to become as successful as we have been.

We are in our eighth year of using data to drive instructional decisions. It was not until the third or fourth year that I began to organize and document the evolutionary process that we were going through on our journey toward improvement. I discovered that this type of documentation was needed when school districts began to ask me what was going on in my district. Trying to explain a DDIS without a model was perplexing. Although what we were doing in my district made perfect sense to me, I found out that it was very difficult to communicate that to other districts in a manner that was easily replicable. When I discovered the need for this type of school improvement model, I decided that creating a model would be the perfect subject for my dissertation. Not only would a DDIS model assist other schools with their initiatives, it would help me make sense of the work we were doing in my own district. A model would help us organize the chaos.

As I contemplated the topic of my dissertation, I literally had a multitude of ideas scribbled across a white board that was approximately 20 feet long. I wanted to write about how other school districts could do what we were doing in my district to achieve success. I knew that what we were doing was making a difference, and I knew that if other districts did the same, they could be successful, too. I wanted to share my journey from the beginning to the present in the hope that it would be valuable to other districts who were seeking to become data driven. How was I going to make sense of all the components in a data-driven system that must work together for success? The question became, where should I begin?

With the help of my dissertation advisor, Dr. Richard Halverson, we made sense of the multitude of components that create a DDIS. The following model was developed at the University of Wisconsin–Madison as I wrote my dissertation.

Figure 1.1 Blink/Halverson Model for Data-Driven Instructional Systems (2005)

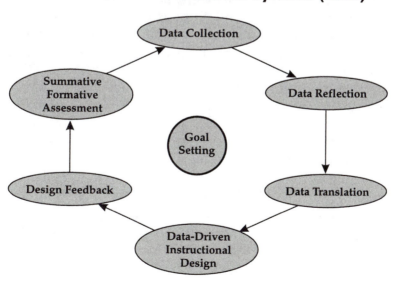

Each component of the DDIS model represents several branches of education that are commonly present in K–12 school districts. Every component of the model has its own chapter in this book. Those chapters provide specific examples, implementation ideas, and suggestions to assist teachers, principals, and school district leaders with the execution of data-driven initiatives. In the pages that follow, I will briefly describe each component and define the scope of the model. By no means does this brief introduction to the components of the DDIS model provide the reader with enough information to implement a DDIS model. The component-specific chapters are designed to provide a step-by step process with examples to help schools and districts move a data-driven school improvement initiative forward in their own district.

Data Collection

School districts that want to move toward a data-driven instructional approach need to understand what data they want to collect and for what purpose. The best way to work through this component is to utilize the work of Dr. Victoria Bernhardt and her four lenses of data collection. Bernhardt's lenses of data include demographic data, perceptions data, student learning data, and school process data. Demographic data include information related to enrollment, attendance, ethnicity, gender, grade level, and English-language proficiency. Who are your students? What do they look like? What are their characteristics? Perceptions data are the values, beliefs, attitudes, and observations of the primary stakeholders in your district, including students, parents, teachers, community members, board members, support staff, instructional paraprofessionals, and administrators. How do the prominent stakeholders in your school district feel about the work that your district is doing? Are they satisfied with the programs that are offered and the academic performance of the students? Student learning data are the results of standardized tests, classroom observations of student achievement, authentic assessments, teacher checklists of student competencies, and any other tools that are used to measure student achievement. How are your students doing on their statewide assessments, local assessments, and classroom assessments? What does performance look like over time? Finally, school process data include information about the school programs and processes that are present in your school system. What programs are available? How are students identified for supplemental or gifted programs? Data should be collected in all of these areas to provide a clear picture of the school district, its students, and their performance.

How does a school or district determine which data to collect in each of the lenses and which data are meaningful to the cause? Create a Data Discovery Team in the district and discuss what types of data should be collected, how often they should be collected, how they will be collected, where they will be stored, how they will be accessed, and who will have access to them. Data collection also involves storing data in a data warehouse and relies heavily on the integration of information technology with the daily operations of schools.

Data Reflection

Data reflection is one of the critical components of the DDIS model but also one of the most difficult to structure. This component is the most complex to organize and requires the biggest shift in district philosophy. Districts have to be ready to focus everything that falls under this component on the use of data at the classroom level. In order to do that, schools need to provide teachers not only with the tools they need to collect data but also with the time they need to analyze and interpret those data. Everything from conferences and workshops to district professional learning days will look different in a DDIS school district. From the time teachers arrive in the morning until they leave at the end of the day, instruction and conversations about instruction must focus on the use of data for student learning.

School districts must realize that professional learning does not drive change—student achievement drives change. What I mean is that, all too often, school districts get stuck in an endless loop of sending teachers to conferences to listen to well-known speakers talk about what has worked in their districts while trying to convince conference attendees they should do the same. Teachers come back from those conferences and want to implement what they have learned. Though that isn't all bad, it is bad if what they want to implement is not what their students need. We typically think of professional learning and student learning in the wrong order. We send teachers off to a conference and expect changes in student achievement after they have implemented what they learned at the conference. In fact, we should be doing the exact opposite: I believe teachers should be analyzing the student learning data they have and determining from that what types of professional learning they need to improve instruction in their classroom, which will eventually improve student achievement levels. However, in most districts that I've worked in or visited, teachers are attending conferences and workshops first and then looking at their data. Figure 1.2 displays the way professional development should be designed around students.

Figure 1.2. Student-Centered Professional Development

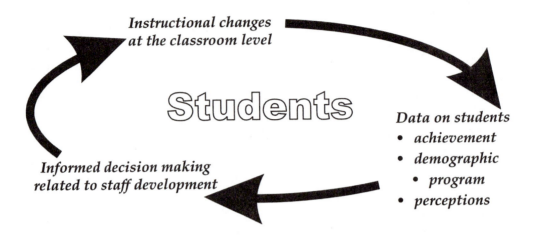

Copyright by Rebecca J. Blink, Ph.D.

For example, I worked in a school district for several years that said it wanted to practice 6 + 1 Trait Writing. For years, when asked whether they were doing 6 + 1 Trait Writing in their schools, teachers and administrators would say that they were. However, when I asked them why they were using 6 + 1 Trait Writing, no one could answer my question. From my point of view, if 6 + 1 Trait Writing is being implemented in a school district, there should be a reason documented with data that explains why that is necessary. If educational leaders can't explain why they are doing some things in their schools, maybe they shouldn't be doing them!

Data reflection makes time for stakeholders to examine data and identify areas in need of improvement. It relates directly to systemic change and school reform. This includes any school improvement planning based on data, and it might include events such as a Data Retreat at which district stakeholders gather to review data findings and address district needs. School districts and buildings within school districts will look different if they use the DDIS model. Unlike a typical school district, using the DDIS model forces districts to start with the data and then move on to analysis and professional learning. Without the DDIS model, professional learning typically comes before any data are analyzed or interpreted—and that is like putting the cart before the horse.

Data Translation

Data translation is the component of the DDIS model that begins to move the data to the instructional level. Data translation includes curriculum mapping, content adjustments, and instructional adjustments. This component of the DDIS model relates to systemic change and school reform, like the data reflection component. Both data reflection and data translation require change at the system level. Data reflection focuses more on changes in the staff culture, whereas data translation refers to actual programming and instructional changes that take place systemically for students. Data translation focuses on a large-scale curricular or program changes within a district.

Again, I will use an example from my own district to illustrate data translation. By analyzing data over several years, it became clear to me that we needed to do something—particularly at the elementary level—to improve our math instruction. Test scores over the past four years had indicated a weakness at our elementary school in a strand of our math standards known as "number operations and relations." Even though we knew that students were performing low in relation to this strand and had talked about it, none of the changes that we made in the classroom had proved successful. Though we had several supplemental support programs in place at the elementary level for reading, we had nothing in place for math. After analyzing the data and determining there were no gaps in the curriculum (what should be taught), I decided to design a supplemental remedial math program based solely on identified student weaknesses on our district math assessment. Students are placed in this program, which we named Math Matters, based on their needs. It is not funded through any federal monies, so students can move in and out of the program as needed. The Math Matters program is a supplemental program in which students receive additional math instruction in 30-minute blocks up to three times per week. This is not an extension of their regular math class. This program was designed strictly to close achievement gaps for students with difficulties in math.

Since its inception in 2003, our Math Matters program has been extremely successful. What used to be a weak area for us on standardized tests—number operations and relations—is no longer a sore spot. We can report that 100% of the students serviced in the Math Matters program as third graders and dismissed at the end of their third-grade year scored proficient or advanced on the math portion of their state assessment after receiving no services over the summer or at the start of their fourth-grade year. To me, that indicates the students serviced in Math Matters not only learned the content but also retained it.

The Math Matters program is one example of data translation in my district. There are many more ways that data can translate into program or curricular changes, and those will be discussed later in this book.

Data-Driven Instructional Design

Data-driven instructional design, which includes the lessons of study and how to teach them, also corresponds with systemic change and school reform. Data-driven instructional design focuses on using data to inform instruction at the classroom level. Unlike data translation, which focuses more on the district and building levels, data-driven instructional design focuses on what is happening in the classroom. As school leaders, we can create all the programs we want, but if we don't change the way teachers teach in the classroom, all the data in the world isn't going to make a difference. Data-driven instructional design is at the heart of the DDIS model. The goal of any data-driven initiative must be to change instruction at the classroom level. The classroom level is where change needs to happen—but it cannot happen without the DDIS model in place to support the efforts of teachers.

Data-driven instructional design refers to the use of data by classroom teachers to plan instructional lessons and activities. This component of the DDIS model requires teachers to design and implement lessons that address the needs of their students. The data that inform instruction come from any number of sources: standardized tests at the state or district level, classroom tests, etc. Teachers must be taught how to use the information they have to create lessons that address the needs of all students in their classroom. Though the concepts taught typically remain the same, the strategies and activities used to teach the concepts differ.

It was at this juncture that my district introduced the concept of tiered lesson planning. Tiered lesson plans require teachers to analyze their classroom data, identify the current performance levels of their students, design lessons to address each child's area of weakness, and teach the lesson to multiple levels of students at once. Examples of tiered lessons are included as Appendices B, C, D, and E.

We spent time training teachers how to look at their data so that they could determine the needs of their students and plan their lessons accordingly. The most important thing to remember when designing the data-driven instructional component of the DDIS model in a district is that teachers do not innately know and understand how to differentiate their instruction. This concept, although they have heard of it, is relatively new to teachers, and they will need training to learn how to do it. Do not assume they know how to do it. When I first saw what were supposed to be tiered lessons in my district, I was very surprised to find out that most of the staff had no idea what I was talking about. At that moment, I knew we needed to do some training. Teachers do not come out of college knowing and understanding how to use data to drive what and how they teach. They have to be taught that skill in a very structured and supportive manner. Because using data at the classroom level is critical to school improvement, training teachers how to do that is essential. Without proper teacher training, data-driven initiatives will stall.

Design Feedback

Design feedback provides information back to teachers, students and administrators regarding the design and progress of school improvement initiatives. This component of the DDIS model encourages the school improvement team to reflect on the progress of the initiative and make any needed adjustments. If teachers are expected to look at data and make adjustments to their instruction based on what they find, so too must the leadership team in a district look at data related to the success or progress of their initiative and make adjustments accordingly. If something is not working, figure out why it is not working. If it is essential to the initiative, figure out how to fix it. If it is not an essential part, get rid of it and create something new.

This component of the DDIS model requires educational leaders in a district to reflect on their own work. This is the time to ask questions. Is the data-driven initiative being driven to the classroom level in such a way that instruction is actually changing based on the data and information that has been gathered? Are classroom teachers changing their instruction to meet the needs of students in such a way that it is making a difference in the level of mastery of content? How is that mastery evidenced in the data? What changes need to be made to sustain the effort and to embed it into the everyday instructional activities of the classroom? Are teachers truly becoming educational leaders in their classroom and demonstrating ownership of the initiative?

Educational leaders and administrators who are leading a data-driven initiative in a school district must be ready to create leaders at the classroom level. Everyone involved in the initiative must be willing to listen to the criticisms of classroom teachers and encourage conversations that may reveal that current practices in a district (no matter how well entrenched) are not working. School districts that are not comfortable providing equal opportunities for all staff members to speak freely should not embark on a data-driven initiative because their culture will not lend itself to the development of a DDIS model. Other models of school improvement would work better in a school district that emphasizes a management style of leadership.

The management style of leadership, in which decisions are made by those in power, does not lend itself to the development of a DDIS model because this model requires feedback and input from all levels in the organization.

Leaders in a school district that is following the DDIS model must be willing to relinquish their power to all stakeholders and to foster a culture that considers all voices as equal partners in the decision-making process. Participants in a data-driven initiative need to be given opportunities to speak openly and voice their opinions without being criticized or having to fear the ramifications of their actions. Educational leaders at the classroom level are critical to the success of this initiative. If a district wants instruction to change at the classroom level, the providers of that instruction—the classroom teachers—need to be on board with this initiative. It is necessary to have candid conversations about the success or failure of any initiative in order to move a school district forward on the data-driven continuum. Until every district reaches 100% proficient or advanced on the statewide assessments in reading and math, every district has room for improvement. "Good enough" are two words that should never be uttered during a school improvement initiative, as they imply that whatever you are doing is not the best. If it is not the best, then there is always room for improvement. Hence, "good enough" clearly implies there is still room for improvement.

No school district can move from good to great without educational leaders at the classroom level. For educational leaders who are used to a managerial style of leadership, this can be uncomfortable. For others, it is just right. It is the latter type of district that will be successful with a data-driven initiative. A DDIS model requires the collaboration and collegiality of a lot of people. Everyone must work together to achieve success. The focus must remain on the data and its impact on student achievement as evidenced through the performance of students.

Summative and Formative Assessment

Summative and formative assessments are conducted to determine the success or effectiveness of the data plan thus far. There are many different types of assessment that can be used to measure whether a system is working and whether students are learning. Summative assessment is defined as an assessment that is given at the end of a unit or chapter to determine whether students have mastered the content taught. Many middle schools and high schools give final exams. These would be considered summative assessments because they are given at the end of a semester or a school year, and their sole purpose is to determine whether students have mastered and remembered the content taught throughout that term. Formative assessments, in contrast, are given to inform instruction. Formative assessments provide classroom teachers with information that they need to change and adjust their instruction to meet the needs of all students. Using formative assessment results, teachers can see the strengths and weaknesses of their students and teach accordingly.

Both summative and formative assessments are necessary and present in school districts—and have been for many years. In school districts that want to be data driven, however, the mind-set of teachers toward assessment must change. Teachers have to stop viewing all assessment as summative. Classroom teachers need to be taught that assessment can be used to help inform their instruction, close achievement gaps, and meet the needs of all students. That piece of professional learning is a critical step in the summative/formative assessment component of the DDIS model. If teachers do not view their assessments as formative, they will not use the data to change what or how they are teaching in the classroom.

Once the assessment is conducted and the results are analyzed and interpreted, goals can be revised, and the whole cycle of the DDIS model begins again. School improvement is a continuous process, and the DDIS model lends itself to the organization and implementation of change because of its cyclical design. The DDIS model assists educational leaders through their continuous improvement efforts by helping them organize what would otherwise seem like unorganized confusion.

Goal Setting and Getting Started

As you look at the DDIS model and begin to conceptualize ways to implement the model in your school district, it is important to note that the goal setting component of the model is fluid. Simply stated, at any time during the utilization of the DDIS model, a goal can be set. For example, if your district is working with the data collection component of the DDIS model and discovers that most of the data entered into the student information systems in each of your district buildings are inaccurate or incomplete, one of your district goals may be to clean up your data-entry processes and procedures. At the same time, your district may look at your state tests results and realize that some improvement in the area of reading needs to be made. So, although the component of goal setting appears stationary in the graphic depiction of the DDIS model (Figure 1.1), it can move in and around the other components of the model as it is being implemented in a school district.

The chapters that follow will describe in detail how educational leaders can design and implement the DDIS model in their own school districts. I will illustrate each component so that you can replicate it in your own district, successfully implement the DDIS model, and become a data-driven school district.

2

Data Collection

The Who, What, Where, When, Why, and How of Data Collection

The first phase of the Data-Driven Instructional System (DDIS) model considers what data are acquired and how data are stored in a school district. Data collection for any school district is a daunting task. Determining what data are necessary to collect and how to collect them is a complete process in and of itself. While researching data initiatives in school districts, I found that the most common challenge cited by administrators was the volume of data in school districts. Literally, folders, boxes, and binders of data are collected and stored within a school district, including multiple copies of state assessment data. Making sense of those data is critical in a data-driven initiative.

The multitude of data collected in school districts can be viewed through four basic lenses: demographics, perceptions, student learning, and school process. In *Data Analysis for Continuous Schoolwide Improvement* (2004), Victoria Bernhardt refers to these four lenses as "multiple measures of data" and argues that it takes several points of data to understand a student's performance. I agree. Most school districts gather and collect data in all four of these data lenses. The four lenses overlap to allow school districts to predict which programs will best meet the needs of all students.

Figure 2.1 (used with permission from Victoria Bernhardt, Ph.D.) clearly shows each of the four data lenses and the overlap between them. The small overlapping area is where the largest efforts in school improvement initiatives take place. Because all four of the data lenses are considered in the overlap, every aspect of data related to a student or a school is taken into account in the development of the school improvement initiative. That small overlapping area is a window of opportunity in which school districts can truly make a difference in the education of their students. Data from the student learning lens related to achievement are considered; data from the demographic lens related to who students are and how they are performing are considered; data from the perceptions lens are considered to understand how students and other stakeholders feel about the district's performance; and data from the school process lens are considered to determine program successes and

13

the need for new programs. When all lenses of the data circles intersect, all aspects of school improvement can be analyzed and reviewed.

Figure 2.1 Multiple Measures of Success

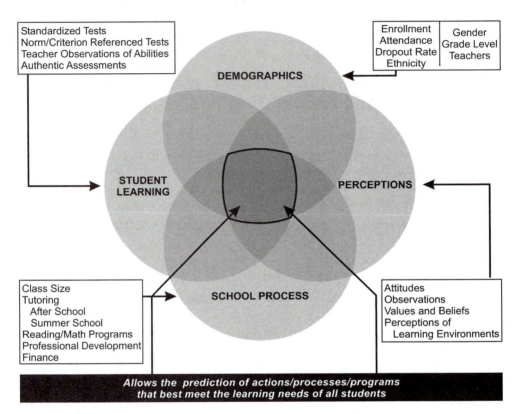

The What and the Why of Data Collection

Demographic Data

Demographic data are typically found in the student information system in a school district. These data are usually collected by building or district-level secretaries and entered into the student information system. Data are collected at all times during the school year and over the summer. These data need to be updated each time a change occurs because the information in the student information system needs to be accurate and timely. Demographic data collected on students should include ethnicity, gender, socioeconomic status, name, Title I status, English-language proficiency, open enrollment data, attendance, courses, discipline, academic grades, health data, special education data, grade-level placement, course schedules, and participation in remedial or enrichment programs.

Student Learning Data

Student learning data are typically found in the student information system in a school district. The data that many districts collect include state and national assessment data, local standardized assessment data, district assessment data, and classroom assessment data. Examples of each data type include the following:

- State and National Assessment Data—Data collected in this area include all state testing information for students in grades 3–8 and grade 10 to meet the requirements of the No Child Left Behind legislation. These data are typically collected once a year after the state assessment is administered and scored when the results are disseminated back to local school districts. For example, ACT scores, SAT scores, PSAT scores, ASVAB scores, NAEP scores, and PLAN scores are all examples of national learning data that are collected in school districts.

- Local Standardized Assessment Data—Data collected in this area include the results of any standardized assessments administered within the district, such as the Northwest Evaluation Association's Measures of Academic Progress (MAP), the Scantron Achievement Series, and the Standardized Test and Assessment of Reading (STAR).

- District Assessment Data (locally assessed)—These data include any assessment data collected from local assessments, such as guided reading level, lexile reading level, running records in reading, qualitative reading inventories, and standards checklists.

- Classroom Assessment Data—Data collected in this area include classroom assessments, common assessments (assessments for the same course regardless of the teacher of record), and classroom or course grades.

These data sources are some examples of what information is collected and used to inform the instructional processes in school districts. These assessments all measure a student's ability and provide information that teachers can use to change the instruction in their classrooms. Teachers and administrators believe that multiple measures of learning are necessary to provide a clear picture of how a child learns. Because these assessments take place throughout the entire school year, the data from these assessments must be collected and analyzed on a regular basis. Student learning data are the most critical data for school improvement. The student learning data tell the story of the success or failure of a school district. Is the educational system currently in place succeeding? How are the students performing? This is the cornerstone of any data initiative.

If students are performing well, the focus of the data-driven initiative is to become even better as a school district. Moving from good to great is never an easy task. If students are not performing well, however, the focus of the initiative is to fix the problem at hand. The natural place to begin fixing anything is to figure out what is causing the problem. The root cause of a problem needs to be identified through the use of data. Often in school districts, we find a program that we think we need and implement it without thoroughly analyzing whether that program meets the needs of the district or the students whom it was designed to assist based on the data collected. At this point, student learning data begins to tell the story of a school district.

School Process Data

School process data include any information that deals with special programs (after school, reading and math, special education, athletics) finance, transportation, or professional learning. Most school districts collect data related to programs and professional learning in conjunction with this data lens and store it in a variety of ways. Some of the data related to this lens is stored in central office buildings or personnel offices. The key to the collection of these data is determining how the information relates to school improvement and student achievement. Does the training of a teacher have an impact on student achievement? Does the time that a student spends on the school bus have an impact on that student's achievement? Do students who participate in athletics or other cocurricular clubs perform better on standardized assessments than students who do not participate in activities outside the regular school day? To answer these questions and to analyze the data at that level, districts need to determine what data they need to gather and why.

For example, if a school district wanted to determine whether the Reading Recovery program (a one-to-one remedial reading program for first-grade students) has been successful in its district, it would have to collect data on which students took part in the program, when they participated in the program, how they performed in classes and on standardized assessments before the program, how they performed in classes and on standardized assessments during the program, how they performed in classes and on standardized assessments after the program, who their teacher was in the program, and how many students who received Reading Recovery are still enrolled in the school district.

For some districts, the collection of these data may involve gathering old class lists from the Reading Recovery teachers to find out which students were in the program and when, collecting old grade books and report card records from past years to determine the classroom performance of those serviced in Reading Recovery, talking with the school district's assessment coordinator to locate any standardized assessment results or state test results, and visiting with building-level secretaries to determine which students who received Reading Recovery are still enrolled in the district. For other districts, all of these data may be kept in a centralized data storage system or a data warehouse.

Finally, once the data are collected, they must be analyzed to find the answer to the original question: Has the Reading Recovery program been successful in our district? What evidence is there to support the conclusion? This is just one example of how data are collected and used to determine program success.

Perceptions Data

Perceptions data are typically overlooked and least likely to be collected in school districts. In working with school districts during data-driven initiatives, I do not believe this data lens is neglected intentionally. Interestingly, school districts are funded by the public, and yet the public is rarely asked to evaluate the job the schools are doing. Of course, the fact that these data are not collected as regularly as demographic data, student learning data, or school process data does not mean they are any less important. It does mean, however, that perceptions data are more difficult to acquire because they require the administration of some sort of written, oral, or online survey; the collection of surveys from people outside the school building (community members, parents, and board members); the tabulation of survey results; and the analysis and interpretation of data. These data are not easily collected within school buildings because they come from people who are not readily available.

Now that the what and why of data collection are a little clearer, let's discuss the who, when, and how. Who should be collecting data in your district? How often should they be collecting it? How are they supposed to collect it—on paper, in a spreadsheet, or in electronic format for importing into a data warehouse?

The Who, When, and How of Data Collection

The most important thing to remember about the collection of data is that someone needs to be in charge. Someone in every school district needs to organize who will collect the data, when the data will be collected, and how the data will be collected. Coordination of the data-driven initiative is critical to its success. In the district where I work and in districts that I have studied, data are collected by many people at different levels. After a person is selected to lead the initiative—the data manager—the best place to start is to create a Data Discovery Team. The data manager needs to investigate who in the district is responsible for collecting data and determine what data each person is responsible for collecting. That list of people and data will guide the creation of the Data Discovery Team.

For example, a school district may have one building secretary in each of its school buildings who is responsible for the collection of demographic data from enrolling families. That secretary would be a member of the Data Discovery Team. The director of curriculum and instruction is typically responsible for collecting data related to standardized assessments. The director of curriculum and instruction would be a member of the Data Discovery Team—and in many cases, he or she will also be the data manager as well. Assistant principals typically collect data related to student discipline. The assistant principal would be a member of the Data Discovery Team. Other members of the Data Discovery Team could include guidance counselors, guidance secretaries, district office secretaries, computer technicians, special education secretaries, building principals, district-level specialists in reading or math, some classroom teachers, and perhaps even the superintendent.

The purpose of the Data Discovery Team is to identify all of the data types and sources that are essential to collect. Through multiple meetings and brainstorming sessions, a complete list of desired types and sources of data, dates when those data will be collected, and the form in which the data will be collected should be determined. The director of curriculum and instruction will demand that all standardized test scores be collected as soon as they are available after the test administration and stored either as paper reports or electronically. Classroom teachers will suggest that their classroom assessment data are critical to improving student achievement and therefore should be collected and stored—probably a minimum of four times per year, to coincide with the quarters of instruction in a school year. The reading and math specialist will insist that his or her student data be collected and stored multiple times a year to help the school make program and instructional changes. The assistant principal will discuss the data he or she has on students and how attendance and behavior referral data can be very helpful in designing school improvement initiatives. The types and sources of data that are identified by the Data Discovery Team need to be documented so that the data manager can begin to formulate a collection plan.

Every person involved in the collection of data in a school system must understand exactly what they are responsible for and how their role in the process is critical. For example, if a building secretary who is responsible for collecting demographic data on enrolling students makes one single mistake (incorrect ethnicity, incorrect gender, incorrect socioeconomic status) in the entry of that data into the student information system, all other data related to that student could be incorrect, and that mistake could invalidate district accountability data collected for No Child Left Behind and adequate yearly progress measures. If a student is listed as Caucasian when he or she is actually Native American, then all of the data related to ethnicity for that school district will be incorrect. One missed keystroke, one field left blank, or one typing error can cause havoc in today's age of accountability and data-driven systems. Though this is only one example of the importance of accurate data entry, it is critical that every member of the Data Discovery Team understands his or her role and the ramifications of one simple mistake.

In my district, one of my roles is that of data manager. It is my responsibility to make sure that the data-driven initiative runs as smoothly as possible, from the first stroke of data entry to the analysis and interpretation of the data. We were struggling with the accuracy of our data entry in all of our school buildings. Because our district has an enrollment of approximately 1,350 students, I could physically check all of our students' records in the student information system, SASIxp (supplied by NCS Pearson). As I looked through the student records, I would find the same mistakes: missing information, information that I knew was incorrect, no ethnicity listed, etc. I found out that the secretaries in the different buildings were entering the data in different ways. Two of the buildings entered students' middle names, whereas one school did not. One school input e-mail addresses for parents, whereas two of the schools did not. We needed to become more uniform in our data-entry procedures. Finally, I decided to create what we call a Data-Entry Protocol (see Appendix A). As a team, we went through every data-entry page in our student information system, documented the fields that should be entered, and gave an example of how it should be entered. For example, it was not enough to say that the address field needed to be entered. We had to instruct secretaries *how* to enter the address field—no abbreviations should be used, the zip code field should be filled (even though the secretaries believed that anyone looking at the data would know the zip code of the city the school was in), and so on. Simple tasks needed to be broken down and demonstrated to eliminate inaccuracies or incompleteness in our data entry. We needed to have everyone in all buildings entering the same data fields in the same way. The registration forms that we used in the school buildings within our district even varied by building. We were not collecting the same information from parents when they enrolled their children. The registration forms needed to be revised so that we were collecting the same information in all of our school buildings.

With the implementation of the Data-Entry Protocol, our data entry became much cleaner and more complete. We still had a few glitches, however. That's when I knew I had to explain the purpose of data collection in a much deeper way than I had in the past. I needed to help everyone understand how critical one keystroke can be in the process of data entry and how one mistake can have serious ramifications in the analysis of the data. Once I shared that information with my Data Discovery Team, the data entry became much more complete and accurate. It is vital for everyone involved in the data-entry process to understand his or her role in the process. I rarely find an incomplete record any more. It might sound as if the process of coordinating and implementing a data-entry process with a Data-Entry Protocol took place in our district in a relatively short time. That's not true. The process I have just described took four years to come to fruition in our school district. Even though we were entering data during that time, we constantly had to look at ways to improve the process. It is only now, four years after the Data-Entry Protocol was first implemented, that I can say more of our data are entered accurately. We are still not error free—but as long as we have humans entering data, we will never be error free.

Part of my job is to check and manage all of the data entry in the systems we have in place. But, you may wonder, how this could be done in a larger district? In talking with other school districts who range in size from 4,000 students to major metropolitan districts that are nearly 100 times our size (135,000 students), I have learned that data collection is a very important component of the DDIS model. Whereas my district has just one person to check approximately 1,350 student records, larger districts may have complete data departments that check the records of their student populations. I often hear that the only reason we can do this "data stuff" is because we are a smaller district. One thing to keep in mind is that people who work in smaller districts often wear multiple hats. By that, I mean that although I have to check the records for all of our students, I also have several other components to my job, including curriculum, instruction, and assessment for the district. In a larger district, multiple people would have to fulfill the roles that I have. Typically, larger districts do have more than one person working with the data for the district. Proportionately, the role of a data manager is the same regardless of the size of the district. Smaller districts have one person managing 1,350 records, whereas larger districts with 135,000 records have a data department (usually part of the information technology staff) that could include as many as 10 employees.

Up to this point, only the data collected and entered on students have been discussed—demographic data and student learning data. These data account for two of the four data lenses that Bernhardt deems necessary for data-driven school districts. These data are only a few of the sources in most school districts. What about the data collected on staff members? What about the data collected on special programs such as Title I or gifted and talented programs? Who is going to collect those data? When is that person going to collect the data, and in what form? All of these questions need to be addressed by the Data Discovery Team to ensure the accuracy and completeness of data collection within a school district.

If your school district believes that teachers have any effect on the success of students, then it must collect data on professional learning—that is, school process data. Why is it that students in one teacher's classroom are more successful than students in another teacher's classroom? How can a district analyze data related to professional learning and relate those data to student achievement? For example, suppose that an elementary school has one fourth-grade teacher whose students consistently score higher than any other fourth-grade classroom in the district on a standardized math assessment. In a data-driven district, administrators need to figure out why that is happening. Is it because the teacher is lucky enough to get all the students who are good in math in his classroom every year? Is it because the teacher attends the state math conference every year and uses the latest best practices research to plan his lessons? Is it because the teacher has 28 years of experience in teaching? A data-driven district that is focused on school improvement seeks to find out why the students in that teacher's classroom perform so well on standardized math assessments and figure out how to replicate that performance in every fourth-grade classroom. If the district determines that the students are performing better because of the knowledge the teacher gained at the state math conference, then the district should send every fourth-grade teacher to the math conference. If the district determines that the teacher is so successful because he or she has 28 years of experience, then the district needs to figure out a way to give all of the fourth-grade teachers a chance to talk with this veteran teacher. Ideally, spending time together as colleagues will enable the veteran teacher to guide and mold less experienced teachers into more confident, experienced teachers. Whatever the case may be, the district needs to figure out why one teacher's students consistently score higher than the students in all other fourth-grade classrooms.

In order to solve that mystery, school districts must track data on the professional learning (courses, workshops, and conferences) of teachers—that is, school process data. Again, the Data Discovery Team should discuss what data need to be collected and who is going to collect those data. Typically, data on professional learning are collected by district office personnel. The data manager needs to determine a process for the collection of professional learning data. That process would outline who is collecting the data, when the data will be collected, and how (in what form) the data will be collected. Once the data are collected, the data manager needs to determine where and how those data will be stored.

To take this process a step further, I believe that professional learning should be based less on what teachers think that they need and more on what the data indicate that students need (refer back to Figure 1.2 on page 6). For example, in one school, sixth-grade teachers felt they should attend professional learning opportunities related to 6 + 1 Trait Writing. However, the data collected indicated that the sixth-grade scores were dropping in reading and that the drop was linked to the students' lack of knowledge of reading strategies. This would indicate that the sixth-grade teachers should attend professional learning opportunities focused on the development of reading strategies for middle-level students, not 6 + 1 Trait Writing. This example demonstrates the use of data to drive professional learning—which is not what typically happens. Too often in public education, we get hooked on the latest and greatest new idea on the market and do not analyze whether we need it. We implement these practices because we think that is what we should be doing, when in reality, we may not need to implement anything new. It is essential that we always look back to the data. What do the data suggest?

One of the most beneficial aspects of using data to drive instructional decisions is the ability to evaluate program effectiveness. Since implementing new programs typically cost school districts money, school boards and district administrators want to know if the newly implemented program is working. The only way to do that is collect and analyze school process data related to the program in question. Have the students who have participated in the program shown improvement? Has the program been cost effective? What evidence is there to support the conclusions? If the students are not demonstrating improvement in the newly implemented program, it would behoove the school district to determine why they were not growing and make the necessary adjustments.

Realizing that data are prevalent in a school district makes one realize just how massive a project the collection and storage of data can be. Once a process for collecting data is formulated, then a school district must decide how it will store all of their data. There are tools that are available to school districts to assist with the storage of data. The most recent tool that has been introduced to public education is the concept of data warehousing. Though data warehousing has been around in the business world for years, school districts have only recently investigated this avenue. My district uses data warehousing software from the TetraData Corporation called *Ease-E Data Analyzer*. Though I believe that data warehousing software is a great tool that can assist with data analysis, it is not necessary for school districts to begin their data-driven initiatives. As long as school districts know what data are being collected, who is responsible for collecting the data, when the data are being collected, how (in what form) the data are being collected, why it is necessary to collect the data, and where the data are being stored, they can move forward using data to drive school improvement.

Getting the data into the hands of teachers and providing them time to review and analyze those data will truly make a difference in any data-driven initiative. According to a teacher in one district I worked with,

> A data system needs to be robust and easily accessible. The data system needs to be really organized on a computer or in a box in a closet; but it needs to be someplace that you can go to and mine for information; it has to involve a lot of people. It just can't be what the guidance department has or just what the administration has, or just what the state test told us. It has to be all of those things plus classroom data, data from colleagues, administrative information, etc. It's a really big thing!

According to one district administrator, "A data system must allow us to look at the data, drill down in different directions, run queries to our advantage to obtain information, and it must contain clean data on which to base decisions." A high school math teacher thought, "The data system must be a way of collecting, compiling, and analyzing the data to improve student achievement." She went on to explain that there are critical components of the data system: "I think collecting, compiling and analyzing are all critical components to the data system because if you don't have a good method of collecting information it won't be accurate; you need to have some method of compiling the information so you have some results; and you certainly need to analyze it or it was not worth collecting."

According to one elementary and middle school principal, "The data system is anything that will accept different forms of data and allow you to prepare that data in different ways." She also pointed out that the condition of the data before it is entered into any system is a critical piece of the process. Several school district employees expressed how important it was for them to have an abundance of data on their students that could be accessed either directly or by contacting an administrator. It was not critical for them to have all of their data in electronic format, but they did require that the data be kept in one place so that all staff members knew where it was and how to access it. They expressed a need for the data to be organized and accurate so that it could be used to make decisions.

Districts must design an organized process of data collection and find a way to get that data into the hands of teachers. Care and caution must be exercised when preparing for the implementation of a data-driven instructional initiative. The data must be entered in the same way in all buildings across the district; the person entering the data must do so with tremendous attention to detail, and the data manager must be able to visualize, create, and implement this complex process in a way that is least cumbersome for everyone.

There is absolutely nothing more critical to the DDIS model for school improvement than the collection and organization of data. If a school district wants to implement a school improvement model focused on the use of data, then the data *must* be accurate and complete. The worst thing a district could do is to be nonchalant about its data collection and organization and move forward with a data-driven initiative. In that scenario, decisions will be made based on inaccurate and incomplete data, which could negate any positive efforts to move the district forward. Once one mistake is made in the analysis of data or one program is changed because of inaccurate data, the credibility of the whole initiative is called into question. Using inaccurate or incomplete data and failing to spend time up front to prepare for this daunting task will sabotage any data-driven instructional system.

Data collection may be only one component of the DDIS model, but it involves much more than the collection of data. Whole processes must be developed within a district to prepare for data collection. Several key points about data collection should be kept in mind:

- Appoint someone in the school district to be the data manager; this person will be responsible for coordinating and organizing the entire initiative.
- Form a Data Discovery Team to discuss the who, what, where, when, why, and how of data collection.
- Determine how and where data will be stored.
- Make sure the district is willing to make a long-term commitment to a school improvement initiative—data-driven initiatives take time to plan and implement.

Finally, do not assume that because data collection is the first component of the DDIS model that it is the easiest to implement. It is the first component of the model because it is the single most important step to ensuring the success of any data-driven initiative.

3

Data Reflection

How and When do Teachers and Administrators Find Time to Analyze and Interpret Data?

Reflecting on district data is vital for improving student achievement. Allowing school district stakeholders time to reflect on the data provides them with the opportunities they need to discuss their findings and plan for improvement. Teachers and administrators, in particular, need to be given opportunities to have conversations about the data they see so that they can determine what should be included in the school improvement plan. Two very distinct, formal opportunities come to mind for teachers and administrators: a three-day Data Retreat and professional learning time. These opportunities allow teachers and administrators time to review their current demographic data, student learning data, school process data, and perceptions data to determine areas of weakness. Once those areas of weakness are identified, these opportunities for data reflection will allow teachers and administrators time to plan for improvement.

District Data Retreat Workshop

A Data Retreat workshop is a three-day intensive opportunity for school district leaders to plan for improvement. These Data Retreats are planned, deliberate activities over the course of three days. The best way to conduct a Data Retreat is to hold it during the summer at an off-site location. I have conducted Data Retreats both in the district and at off-site locations; holding the retreat at an off-site location limits the distractions that typically surface when teams of administrators and teachers conduct a meeting in one or more of their district buildings. Data Retreats follow a format developed by Judy K. Sargent, Ph.D. (2006), the school improvement coordinator for a state regional education office in Wisconsin, and can be customized by local school districts to meet local needs.

The Data Retreat follows an eight-step process of analysis over three days:

◆ Step 1: Team Readiness—Prior to the retreat, the characteristics of effective teams are defined, ground rules are set, and roles are assigned to team members. Characteristics of effective teams include the following:

Setting a clear vision of outcomes

Using data to confirm or reject perceptions

Honoring the privacy of student, staff, and family information

Setting and following ground rules for effective meetings and group work

Sharing responsibility for every student in the school

Following the characteristics of professional learning communities

Moving from a convenience and historical orientation to a results orientation in order to make decisions

Thoroughly analyzing and interpreting data to guide decision making

Collecting the data needed to evaluate school effectiveness

- Step 2: Identifying Data Sources—This step can also be conducted prior to the Data Retreat. Data sources are identified within the district, discussion focuses on which data are relevant and where those data will be stored.

- Step 3: Data Analysis—This step takes up the entire first day and part of the second day of the retreat. It is important to include the analysis of data at the retreat so that all District Leadership Team members are a involved in the process. Data are analyzed using Bernhardt's four data lenses—demographic data, student learning data, school process data, and perceptions data.

The second day of the Data Retreat continues to focus on data analysis but moves into subgroup analysis and discussion of data management. On the third and final day of the Data Retreat, Steps 4 and 5 are completed:

- Step 4: Making Hypotheses and Identifying Issues

- Step 5: Prioritizing and Setting Improvement Goals

After the Data Retreat, Steps 6, 7, and 8 provide the culminating experience for the entire process:

- Step 6: Designing Objectives and Strategies—this step will assist the district in meeting its goals.

- Step 7: Progress Monitoring and Evaluation—this step forces the district to develop a plan that will encourage monitoring through data, which will help keep the district on the path toward improvement.

- Step 8: Making a Commitment and Planning for "Roll Out"—this step will ensure the sustainability of the improvement plans created at the Data Retreat. How will the information discovered at the Data Retreat be shared with the entire staff?

During the Team Readiness step of the Data Retreat process, a District Leadership Team is formed. The District Leadership Team is essential to the Data Retreat process. A school district must determine who should be involved in the Data Retreat. The District Leadership Team should be representative of the school staff and administration and should represent all subgroups outlined under the No Child Left Behind legislation. Typical participants might include building-level principals, curricular department heads, grade-level representatives, special education representatives, guidance counselors, English-language learning coordinators, curricular specialists, the director of curriculum and instruction, the district assessment coordinator, and the district administrator. The District Leadership team should include district employees who have the capability to become leaders among their peers. Routinely, building administrators select the District Leadership Team members from their own buildings. District-level administrators are automatically members of the District Leadership Team. Careful attention must be paid to the selection of the District Leadership Team, as these people will be asked to drive school improvement initiatives and implement building improvement plans with their colleagues after the Data Retreat. It is critical that the members selected are people whom other teachers will follow. They have to be leaders among their peers.

With that responsibility comes a caution: Administrators who do not want to create teacher-leaders in their building should not become part of a data-driven initiative. Members of the District Leadership Team have to be willing to say what they believe at all costs, without fear of ramifications or retaliation from the school administration. Everyone on the District Leadership Team—teachers, administrators, guidance counselors, or district administrators—should be considered equal partners on the team. If administrators are reluctant to listen to what the District Leadership Team members say, they should not be creating leaders. That sounds a little harsh, but in order for a District Leadership Team to do its job effectively, all members of the team have to feel as if they can say whatever they want and have their opinions matter just as much as any other member of the team. There must be mutual respect among all members so that teachers feel just as much at ease stating their opinions as administrators do.

A second caution related to the District Leadership Team is that everyone on that team must be willing to look at and analyze data—no matter what the data suggest. If, for example, the data suggest that students in a high school are performing at lower levels in reading since the implementation of a block schedule three years ago, then the concept of block scheduling needs to be examined to a deeper level. Teachers who have been supportive of the block schedule all along cannot take offense to the fact that their schedule is being scrutinized. The high school principal, who has sung the praises of the block schedule to the members of the school board and community, must be willing to take a deeper look at the program based on the analysis of data. Emotional ties to programs and people must be checked at the door when a district conducts a Data Retreat. Everyone involved must enter the experience with an open mind and be willing to criticize things that they may have designed or implemented themselves. The data will tell the story to anyone who is willing to listen and evaluate.

Prior to the actual Data Retreat workshop, the District Leadership Team should address several issues during the Team Readiness step. First, the purpose and vision of the Data Retreat must be established: Why has your district decided to hold a Data Retreat? What do you hope will happen as a result of attending the Data Retreat? What outcomes does your District Leadership Team hope to accomplish by attending the Data Retreat? (Sargent, 2006).

Second, the District Leadership Team needs to understand that the data they are about to review will either confirm or reject their own perceptions, and they must be willing to objectively analyze information that may contradict their own personal beliefs. During this step, it may be helpful to have the District Leadership Team write down or discuss their perceptions. How do they think the students are performing? What are the district's strengths and weak areas? Which subgroups are most at risk? (Sargent, 2006). Save those perceptions until the end of the Data Retreat workshop to see how close to reality they are.

Third, every member of the District Leadership Team must understand and respect the protocol of confidentiality. Because very detailed data on students, families, and other confidential areas will be discussed during the retreat, every person in attendance must realize that specific data cannot be discussed outside the company of the education professionals at the Data Retreat workshop (Sargent, 2006).

Fourth, ground rules must be set up to govern the work of an effective team. In order for a District Leadership Team to have candid discussions about school improvement, every participant must be willing to share his or her opinion without fear or reservation. People will disagree, and discussions will get heated. Establishing ground rules will help extinguish adversarial situations should they arise.

Fifth, discuss the concept of shared responsibility at the Data Retreat workshop. Successful schools understand that all staff share responsibility for every student in the building (Sargent, 2006).

Sixth, professional learning communities need to be a embedded in the culture of the school district in order to succeed with a data-driven initiative

(Sargent, 2006). As a District Leadership Team, discuss the characteristics of a professional learning community and identify which ones your district exhibits.

Finally, the District Leadership Team needs to understand that it will be called upon to drive the data-driven initiative in the district and to move the district to define itself as results oriented. As a team, discuss examples of situations in which the district has already acted in a results-oriented fashion and ways in which your district can improve.

The second step in the Data Retreat process—Identifying Data Sources—should also be conducted prior to the retreat. Once the types and sources of relevant data are identified, they must be collected and stored in a manner that will be easily accessible during the Data Retreat workshop. Data from all four lenses of Bernhardt's multiple measures of success should be collected in preparation for the Data Retreat. These data include information related to demographics, student learning, school processes, and perceptions.

The third step in the Data Retreat process, Data Analysis, is the first step that should be completed during the Data Retreat. Seven modules can be analyzed during this step: literacy, math and science, safety and health, high schools, special education, early learning, and English-language learning. A school district can work through all of the modules, or just the ones that are most pertinent to its schools. During the analysis, data should be displayed in the form of tables and graphs. District Leadership Team members should observe the data and document any patterns they notice. The team should then formulate hypotheses related to the data findings and document any immediate thoughts they have for improving classroom instruction.

Step 4, Making Hypotheses and Identifying Issues, is the stage of the retreat when the hypotheses developed throughout the Data Retreat process are refined and issues related to school improvement are raised. The final list of hypotheses should be plausible explanations of practice that may have contributed to the observed results (Sargent, 2006). In effective decision making, the issues should be stated and clarified by all members of the team (Sargent, 2006).

Improvement Goals, Step 5, are the bridge between data analysis and school improvement planning. Members of the District Leadership Team should spend some time quietly reflecting on all of the hypotheses developed during the Data Retreat process. After a period of reflection, the team should prioritize the issues that are in front of them and decide which ones they want to develop into goals for the school district. Then the District Leadership Team should work together to develop a clear, measurable goal for their district or building for the upcoming school year.

Figure 3.1. Moving from Data Analysis to School Improvement Planning

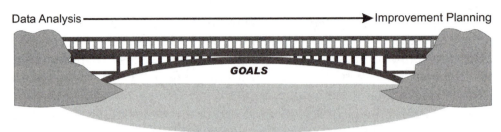

Step 6 in the Data Retreat process is Designing Objectives and Strategies. During this phase of the Data Retreat, District Leadership Team members must work on the details of their district or school improvement plan (Sargent, 2006). The team needs to determine what will be done, when it will be done, how it will be done, who will do it, and with what resources. During this planning, the District Leadership Team must keep in mind how they will measure the objectives and strategies they want to incorporate into their goal. Keeping the measure in mind often helps to plan the process leading up to the measure. As issues are being discussed and incorporated into the improvement plan, concerns brought up earlier in the Data Retreat process need to be addressed. It is not enough to say that we need to improve reading achievement in our school. We need to clarify that by saying we need to improve reading achievement in grades 2, 3, and 4 through the use of differentiated instruction, data analysis, and the implementation of a high school tutoring program that provides after school tutors to struggling students. The District Leadership Team has to saturate the discussion with as many possible causes for an issue as they can. In order to correct an issue and improve student achievement, it is absolutely necessary to get to the root of the problem. As the discussion progresses, the issues can be grouped by category. Place all the issues that deal with organizational or systemic constraints in one group. Place all the issues that deal with staff, money, and resources in a second group, and so on. The categories will be developed during the Data Retreat process, and every district's issues will be different. In my district, for example, I may have issues in reading that relate more to funding than anything else. In your district, the issues may be related more to diversity than to funding.

Figure 3.2. Documenting Your District/School Improvement Plan

Objective	Task	Cost	Person Responsible	People Involved	Date of Task Completion					Monitor
					Sept	Oct	Nov	Dec	Jan	

(Sargent, 2006)

Figure 3.2 shows one way to begin documenting your district/school improvement plan. Having a documented plan as your district heads into the next school year will keep your school improvement plan focused on the goals set during the Data Retreat.

Progress Monitoring and Evaluation is Step 7 in the Data Retreat process. Planning for progress monitoring and evaluation of a school improvement plan is essential. If monitoring and evaluation are not a critical part of the planning process, the follow-through related to the school improvement plan often does not occur. If it is not planned for and time is not specifically allotted for monitoring and evaluation, it does not happen. Once school starts again in the fall, everyone gets busy doing things in their classrooms, and before you know it, no one is monitoring or evaluating the success of the school improvement plan. Monitoring and evaluation should clearly identify tasks and specify who is to complete them, estimate the anticipated costs, and establish a timeline for completion. The District Leadership Team should meet periodically to discuss the progress of the school improvement plan and to monitor and evaluate its success. Don't wait until the end of the school year to discuss the school improvement plan. If it is discussed throughout the school year, it can be adjusted as needed. Perhaps something is not working as well as predicted, or perhaps a goal was met earlier than planned. At those moments, it is time to adjust the school improvement plan.

The final step in the Data Retreat process is Roll Out and Sustainability. The final part of the school improvement plan must account for a continued focus, as a building and as a district, on the needs identified during the Data Retreat. How will the District Leadership Team help the rest of the staff take ownership of the plan? How will the staff engage with the data? How will the District Leadership Team engage the staff in discussions, observations, hypotheses, and ideas? How will the staff be connected to the goals? How will the staff be included in the improvement of education for all students and embedded in a culture of improvement? This is the time to discuss how all staff will be involved in the improvement plan, including teachers of noncore academic classes such as technology education, music education, art education, business education, physical education, family and consumer education, and vocational education. How will the teachers of those subjects find meaning in the school improvement plan as it relates to their academic areas?

At the end of the Data Retreat, it is important to celebrate the work that has just been accomplished. Planning for school improvement is hard work, and it should be recognized by the district and its leaders. Celebrate the success of the Data Retreat while inspiring those in attendance to be leaders in their buildings. Use this opportunity to unleash the power of data as the guiding force for school improvement. Empower others to take the message forward with the same enthusiasm they now feel after completing an intense Data Retreat workshop.

A Data Retreat can be facilitated by a member of the District Leadership Team or by an outside facilitator. My district has conducted them both ways. For the first four years, we used an outside facilitator; for the last two years, I have facilitated our Data Retreats. The best way to conduct a Data Retreat depends on the district. However, it is imperative to understand the process of the Data Retreat workshop prior to facilitating your own. (The Data Retreat workshop is a registered service mark of Cooperative Educational Service Agency 7, Green Bay, Wisconsin. All materials needed to attend or conduct a workshop can be found at http://www.cesa7.k12.wi.us/newweb/content/schoolimprove/data_retreats.)

The Data Retreat provides school districts with more focused school improvement plans for their buildings and for the district overall. School improvement plans developed through the cooperative efforts of the teachers and administrators at the Data Retreat have more momentum because several people in each building in the district have a vested interest in the plan they helped create. Improvement plans that are developed by a team of teachers and administrators from every building also demonstrate collegiality to the board of education, encouraging them to adopt the school improvement plans with little or no discussion.

The use of the Data Retreat workshop has evolved over time. One administrator in the Barkdale (Wisconsin) School District noted, "Originally, we were working with our state regional education office, and the Data Retreats were simply a reflection on state testing, but now we've tried to reflect also on our MAP [Measures of Academic Progress] data and in fact, we are now trying to write our goals based off of the MAP data rather than off the state test data." Barkdale moved from using the Wisconsin Knowledge and Concepts Exam (WKCE) data to the MAP data because the latter measure student growth, whereas the state testing data measure system accountability. The WKCE is the state assessment given in the fall (October/November) to all students in grades 3–8 and grade 10. The MAP exams are computer-adaptive tests developed for Wisconsin (and many other states) by the Northwest Evaluation Association. The MAP assessments measure a student's growth or progress over time, whereas the WKCE assessment is a measure of accountability given only once a year to meet the requirements of the No Child Left Behind Act.

In Barkdale, the MAP assessments are used in a much more formative way than the state assessment. the district's teachers and administrators believe that if they improve students' scores on the MAP assessments and base their improvement goals on that objective, the WKCE scores will take care of themselves. Before implementing the MAP assessments in Barkdale, the WKCE state test results did play a more formative role. However, since the implementation of the MAP assessments, the WKCE has taken on a much more summative role, and MAP provides the formative data needed to develop school improvement plans. This change has been embraced by the teachers in the district because they can adjust their instruction in the classroom in a much more timely manner.

Unlike the WKCE assessment data reports, the MAP reports allow teachers to reflect more formatively on the data to determine what specifically needs to be improved in a particular area of study. Differentiating between the assessment data reported from the administration of the WKCE and that reported from the MAP is somewhat like reading a novel, according to one Barkdale High School English teacher. She said,

> It's like reading a novel. If you read it through once, you get the story but then if you read it through again, you can start pulling out pieces that are important and finding the information and the quotes to support the theme or whatever happens to be in it. It's the same way with the data. You read through it once to see what it says and then you start getting ideas. Then you go back to see if you can prove them. So it is kind of like a scientific experiment. It really, really, really, really helps to have multiple people involved with the data so I can start throwing out ideas or somebody else can throw out ideas and then another person grabs it and runs with it or disproves it – whatever it happens to be. It is definitely one of those cases where two or three or four heads are definitely better than one.

The implementation of the MAP assessments in the Barkdale School District changed the way the district's Data Retreat was conducted. Teachers and administrators have moved away from analyzing only the state test data to include assessment data from the MAP tests. Because the MAP data provide districts with more formative data, the opportunities to use these data to effect instructional change in the classroom are endless. Barkdale is moving in that direction, but it is not there yet. Though there are a few examples of the use of MAP data as a formative tool to change instruction, that mind-set has not yet become embedded in Barkdale's school culture.

My school district has gone through a similar metamorphosis in relation to the Data Retreat. I will never forget the first time the district administrator told the rest of us that we were going to attend this thing called a Data Retreat. All of the other administrators looked at each other as if she were kidding herself. However, as the story goes, the district administrator held her ground, and that summer, the whole administrative team from my school district attended a Data Retreat. The only data that we really evaluated and analyzed that first year were the WKCE assessment data. That was all the data we had at the time.

Since that first Data Retreat, our district has evolved tremendously. The second year, we took a team of teachers and administrators to the Data Retreat, and the administrators brought more data with them. We had two years of MAP assessment data, which we analyzed alongside the state assessment data. At that Data Retreat, the teachers and administrators started to identify patterns of achievement in the data. They saw that students tended to score the same or nearly the same on the WKCE and the MAP assessments. Because the MAP assessments can be given early in the year, this was a wonderful discovery. If the assessments could be given early enough to provide teachers with data on their students right away, perhaps by the time the WKCE test rolled around, the teachers would have been able to help the children whom they had identified as being at risk early in the school year.

At the third Data Retreat we attended, the district's data warehouse unveiled. That was the last year we used the regional state education agency to assist with the Data Retreat process. According to our district administrator,

> The teachers and other administrators were totally engrossed in the data. They kept our director of curriculum and instruction/district assessment coordinator busy running queries to test new theories that they were developing based on the data. They moved beyond what the data said to wonder why something was happening. The staff had spread their wings far enough now that it was time for us to see if they could fly on their own.

We had traditionally been attending a Data Retreat facilitated by the regional state education agency, but during the summer of 2004, our school district conducted its own Data Retreat. We had attended the Data Retreats at the state regional education agency for about four years, but after implementing a data warehouse, the teachers in our district wanted to dig deeper into the data. We could not do that when the facilitator was working with other districts—we were getting way ahead of the other districts. We decided to host our own retreat, and now I am the facilitator of the annual Data Retreat.

A high school math teacher in his third year in our school district contrasted his former district with ours when he spoke about the Data Retreat workshop:

> Having representatives from every school in the district get together and talk about the data overall and then break it down into individual schools and grade levels to identify strengths and areas in need of improvement is something I have never experienced be-

fore coming here. We did not do that in my last district. Being a part of this experience and seeing that we are actually making decisions as far as what we do on a curriculum basis based on the data that we have been gathering and based on our Data Retreats in the summertime, I would say that shows that the district is data-driven. We have the data first of all, and then we are given the time to reflect on it and digest it. We have the ability to make changes based on that data.

It is critical to involve members of the teaching staff in the Data Retreat process. We learned how to improve the Data Retreat experience as the years went by, and recently, we hosted our own Data Retreat with a District Leadership Team of more than 20 employees. It is also essential for this Data Retreat team to include teachers of special education students. Teachers take the data back to the district and share it with their colleagues. They share their experience with those who did not attend and explain how they arrived at the hypotheses they did. Then the Data Retreat team members are asked to share the school improvement plans that were developed at the summer Data Retreat. The action plans for accomplishing the goals listed on the school improvement plan are also rolled out to the full staff. The information from the Data Retreat that is shared with the entire staff on the first professional learning day after summer vacation is the focal point for the rest of the school year. The plans are monitored several times throughout the year for progress and revision.

As the examples both of these districts illustrate, a Data Retreat workshop can look different in each district. How it is organized and where it takes place is up to the district. However, the eight-step process is the best way to ensure a critical analysis of all data needed to develop school and district level improvement plans that are data driven.

Professional Learning Time

Another formal opportunity for data reflection in a school district involves the use of professional learning time. Every district across the country has professional learning days built into the school calendar. What a data-driven school district does with those days needs to be extremely focused and aligned with its vision. Like everything else in a data-driven school district, professional learning time needs to be focused on data and data use. Too often, school districts use these days as an opportunity to bring in speakers to motivate and energize teachers. The problem is that once the initial enthusiasm wears off from the speaker's presentation, the day-to-day operations of the school building revert to the way they have always been. Because all districts build these days into their yearly calendars, districts that want to be data driven need to grab those days and focus their activities on what the data suggest is needed. In my opinion, professional learning opportunities need to be focused less on what teachers think they need and more on what the data suggest that students in the classroom need. All too often, we design our professional learning on the latest best practices in education, regardless of whether the implementation of that best practice is warranted in our district.

A Typical Professional Learning Scenario

A school district has a professional learning day. It brings in a motivational speaker who talks about what a difficult job teaching is and how public education has changed over the last 10 years. The speaker talks about teaching the standards and how the latest research on best practices in education can meet the needs of all students. Some of the topics the presenter cover are guided reading, professional learning communities, standards-based assessment, and working with English-language learners in the regular content classroom. After hearing this presenter, the teachers are excited and anxious to implement guided reading practices at the elementary level; the teachers at the middle school level want to investigate standards-based assessments; and the high school teachers want to design and implement a professional learning community. The district moves forward with the implementation of three different ideas at three different levels. Guided reading becomes the focus at the elementary level, standards-based assessments are the focus at the middle school level, and professional learning communities are the focus at the high school level. Each building moves ahead with its individual focus.

A Data-Driven Professional Learning Scenario

A school district has a professional learning day. Before the professional learning day, all of the teachers in this district have given an assessment, and they know that the data suggest a need for more standards-based assessments. The school district brings in several companies that are knowledgeable about standards-based assessments and offer tools that can be used by all staff members in the district. Every teacher is exposed to several systems of evaluation. After the demonstrations, the teachers meet in grade-level and content teams to determine which system or tool would be most useful in addressing their need for standards-based assessment. The full staff regroups at the end of the day and a decision is made as to which tools the district will use to move forward. There is one vision, one goal, based on data.

Both scenarios depict professional learning opportunities that could occur anywhere the country. One district has a myriad of questions and ideas after hearing a motivational speaker. The other district has a focused professional learning day structured around identified needs in their data. A data-driven school district has to be diligent about keeping the focus on the data and on the needs of the students. The priority in data-driven school districts must be to provide professional learning opportunities for teachers that are directly linked to the performance of the students in their classrooms for the sole purpose of improving student achievement.

Another formal opportunity for teachers and administrators in the schools in my district to reflect on data occurs on early release days. Four half days per school year are dedicated to the analysis and interpretation of data. These days are planned throughout the year and typically follow the administration of standardized assessments, so the data the staff are reviewing are current and timely. These early release days comprise specific tasks that are created by the administrative team. I develop an agenda for each early release day and present it to the full administrative team. Once approved, that agenda is sent to all instructional staff. Typically, the tasks to be completed are included with the agenda for the instructional staff to use as models. At the end of each early release day, each instructional staff member is expected to turn in a completed task for the day using his or her own classroom data. It is the responsibility of the building-level principals to follow through with the instructional staff to ensure that the completed tasks are carried out in the classrooms.

One example of an early release day agenda is the completion of a tiered lesson. An example of a tiered lesson is included later in this book (Appendix B). In this activity, teachers are expected to look at the latest achievement data for the students in their classroom and create a lesson that meets the needs of all students based on the most recent data available to them. Another example of an early release day task is a review of standards calendars. Each core academic area has a standards calendar in my district. These calendars list the Wisconsin Model Academic Standards for which classroom teachers are responsible. Time is given on an early release day for teachers to update and revise their calendars, indicating which standards they have covered and assessed and which standards they have yet to cover. The standards are not usually covered in order because of adjustments made to instruction based on data. Teachers teach what students need to learn, not necessarily what is next in the textbook or on the standards calendar. These activities are purposefully designed to gently encourage teachers to differentiate their delivery of instruction within their classroom to meet the needs of all students. Talking about the early release days, a middle school reading teacher in my district said, "Those half days are really helpful. They are devoted to data tasks that we are supposed to be working on and it helps me."

The Barkdale School District implemented weekly collaboration days several years ago. The administrators and teaching staff in Barkdale proposed to the school board that they have one afternoon off per week for professional learning time. They had a structured agenda in place for each of the collaboration days for every week of the school year. They are now in their third year of this process and find the time very beneficial. Not only do they use this time to reflect on their data, they use it to move the data-driven initiative forward in their district, as well as to complete activities that will drive the data analysis to the classroom level. Admittedly, this weekly collaboration time started out as too structured. The district administrator shared with me that the group had too many things planned for the year. After the first year, the teachers complained that they didn't have time to go into each issue in as much depth as they would like because too many things needed to be accomplished during that time. Now, Barkdale staff members help plan the weekly collaboration days, which allows a slower, more thorough pace that is acceptable to the teaching staff.

Other, more informal opportunities for data reflection may also exist in school districts, such as team planning time, weekly or monthly staff meetings, monthly department meetings, monthly reading and math meetings, District Leadership Team meetings, administrative meetings, board of education meetings, and committee meetings. Each and every time people gather together, part of their purpose for meeting should include reflection on data and data sources throughout the district.

There are several ongoing, informal ways that we reflect on data in my district. The district administrator has summarized some of these informal ways:

> Our prep time or our teacher planning time schedule has changed dramatically because data has indicated to us that we need to put teachers together. As a result, when we have put teachers together I think it's starting to show that we get the teachers to start talking and looking at the data because they are making instructional changes that are good for kids and they are making the student achievement initiative much better.

The middle school principal concurs with the district administrator. He says, "I think the data are brought out and openly discussed with staff. We are getting to the point now that this is more driven from the bottom up. It's not just being forced by the administrators. It is staff recognizing situations and/or opportunities to improve what we are doing and that has been a giant stride for us."

Reflecting on data must be embedded in the daily routine, and it must become a part of the school culture. Teachers, administrators, and students need to be constantly talking about achievement and how to improve it. Students in the district where I work were overheard talking with a representative visiting our schools from the U.S. Department of Education. They said, "We aren't very good athletes here, but we are smart kids, and we like it that way." They are extremely proud of what they can and have accomplished. That feeling of pride permeates all of the school buildings in the district.

In the Barkdale School District, data reflection also occurs in ongoing, informal settings. The informal opportunities are a part of building-level staff meetings and team planning time. Looking at data to improve student achievement has become a part of who the school personnel are in Barkdale. One high school math teacher said it best when he stated, "We have Data Retreats and collaboration time, but sometimes we just do it on our own time—at night or whenever—because it just has to be done."

Analyzing and interpreting data must become something that teachers and school personnel do every day in a data-driven school district because they believe it is the right thing to do to improve student achievement. The school culture and district expectations play a key role in the implementation of a data-driven system. Teachers and administrators in data-driven districts find the time to reflect on their data, either in a systemwide, formal way provided by the school district or in an ongoing, informal way determined by each person. No matter how the reflection takes place, formally or informally, teachers and administrators in data-driven districts are constantly reviewing their data and basing decisions on what they find.

4

Data Translation

How and When Are the Data
Translated Into Program and Curriculum Changes?

Translating the district data into content, curriculum, and program revision is the step in the Data-Driven Instructional System (DDIS) model that will determine how and in what areas the data will affect instruction at the classroom level. Data translation is tied closely to data-driven instructional design in school districts, and it is evidenced by visible changes within school buildings. Although data translation and data-driven instructional design are two separate components of the DDIS model, they are closely related to each other. One provides the ways in which to accomplish change at the program or service level (data translation), whereas the other demonstrates the actual changes that have taken place at the classroom or instructional level (data-driven instructional design).

Data translation in the Barkdale School District was evidenced by the addition of several new initiatives. One such initiative took place at Barkdale High School. At the district Data Retreat during the summer of 2003, data on gender were analyzed and interpreted. Data Retreat participants from the Barkdale School District identified an achievement gap based on test data from both the Wisconsin Knowledge and Concepts Exam (WKCE) and the Measures of Academic Progress (MAP) assessments in the areas of science and English composition at the high school level. The school's director of curriculum and instruction summarized,

> We really took a look at the gender equity or inequity and the performance of the two gender groups. Right away, we set forth actions that we could take during the 2003–04 school year or that we could set into place for the 2004–05 school year. Last year, the high school staff said that they wanted to meet with boys and girls at every grade level and just talk about what they were doing, what their goals were, how they viewed themselves, and really have an open dialogue between the students and the teachers. Leaders of the teaching staff met with groups of students and conducted discussions with groups of students who were separated by gender.

The meetings consisted of candid discussions with students, during which teachers stated that the national achievement data suggested that males perform higher than females in science and math, whereas females performed better in English and language arts–related subjects. "These conversations were used as a pep talk prior to the administration of the state assessments and the thought was that making students aware of the expectation of lower performance in certain areas would motivate those students to try harder in the areas in which their gender was not as successful," the director of curriculum and instruction clarified.

From those discussions with students, a pilot program was instituted at Barkdale High School during the 2004–05 school year. The principal explained the new pilot program in detail:

> After conducting gender specific discussions with groups of high school students, it became evident to us that we needed to do something different in the area of instruction in our science and English departments at the high school level. Beginning in the fall of 2004, we created courses for freshmen in science and English that are gender specific. By that I mean, that freshmen boys are separated from freshmen girls in their science and English classes. We are going to try this for a minimum of three years to see if it has any impact on the achievement gap that we identified at a Data Retreat during the summer of 2003 between males and females in science and English classes. We would have started this sooner, but by the time we got back from the Data Retreat in the summer of 2003, the courses for the 2003–04 school year were already set. We decided to implement this gender course change in the fall of 2004. We are currently in our second year of this program.

Another example of data translation in the Barkdale School District was the addition of a four-year-old kindergarten program beginning in the fall of 2004. The director of curriculum and instruction explained,

> Another example of our use of data was the 4K program. We were able to push for this program because through the data analysis with teachers and looking at what the kids were coming to us with and still struggling in kindergarten and first grade—those first heavy-hitting foundational years—we knew we needed kids across the board to have exposure to a structured and consistent early childhood program. Prior to implementing our 4K program, we had students coming in for a prekindergarten program that consisted of one two-hour session a week—that was it. They were here either on a Tuesday or a Thursday for either the morning or the afternoon for two hours. When I first came here, I squawked

about that a little bit and the program moved to having the students come in on Tuesdays and Thursdays. So then they were getting four hours of structured time. However, the program was still just for students who had been identified as being delayed. We needed to find a way to get all students involved in this program. We were able to make a proposal to the board, do the research, provide the data two years ago to the board and the public, and implement our first full-time 4K program in the district in the fall of 2004 and I'm thrilled. There is an instance where the data really promulgated a new program and a need for it. Now we are going to monitor and look at it. Are the kids going to be more prepared for kindergarten and better performing at the end of kindergarten as a result of this program? We'll see.

A second-grade teacher in the Barkdale School District viewed the use of data in her district as a way to focus the curriculum. She said, "I think we've had to be very meticulous when it comes to curriculum. With all of the testing that is coming from the federal government and the state standards, the basis of a good school is a good curriculum. The data make us look at our curriculum and identify where we are weak and where we are strong. We can't just walk into a classroom and teach whatever we want."

In my school district, we have also made multiple curriculum revisions, content revisions, and instructional adjustments since the implementation of a data-driven system. One middle school math teacher who is also the math department chairperson explained that several changes had been made to the math curriculum as a result of data analysis. She commented,

> From first grade through seventh grade, we did two very specific things related to data and programming changes. We sat down last year and, based on the data, we analyzed where things fall in the school year and we changed the sequencing of the material based on the need. The weaker areas are taught earlier in the year and reinforced throughout the year and the strengths are put off more toward the end of the year just to be reviewed. That is something that we did as a math department looking from the elementary on up. I think it is going to be very helpful because people were teaching Chapter 1, Chapter 2, Chapter 3 and some of those books have 36 chapters. They would get to Chapter 16 and be done for the year because the year was over. Usually, the meat and potatoes came later in the book and we were not getting to it all. The data was showing us that we needed to get to it all. Textbooks are resources; they are not the curriculum. Now teachers teach what they [students] need based on the data and skip around in their textbook.

We do make sure all of the standards are covered and the weakest areas are hit the hardest. The second thing we did was an area of emphasis at each grade level. Every grade level from first through sixth is responsible for one emphasis area that is taught daily. First grade has addition, second grade has subtraction, third grade has multiplication, fourth grade has division, fifth grade has decimals, and sixth grade has fractions. Every day, each grade level does a mini-lesson with their emphasized basic math concept. That way the students are getting the repetition they seem to need in some cases. Those two things went into place last fall and the data has shown tremendous improvement in student performance as a result.

Another major change in my district was made in the middle school math curriculum. During the 2001–02 school year, the middle school math curriculum consisted of fifth-grade math, sixth-grade math, seventh-grade math, eighth-grade math, and one section of algebra in the eighth grade. In order for seventh-grade students to be placed into eighth-grade algebra, they had to have a letter grade of A in each quarter and must not have missed any assignments. The seventh-grade math teacher bore the full responsibility of placing students into the eighth-grade algebra class based on their performance in his seventh-grade math class.

After spending a tremendous amount of time analyzing the state test data, implementing the MAP assessments, and studying those data, we decided to make some changes. We discovered that we were not challenging students enough in math, evidenced by the fact that their scores were reaching a plateau on the state exam. Starting with the 2002–03 school year, the eighth-grade math curriculum began to change. Our middle school went from having one section of algebra to having three sections, and students were placed into algebra based on their quarterly grades, MAP test data, and teacher recommendations. This decision was no longer the responsibility of one individual. During the 2003–04 school year, a section of algebra was added at the seventh-grade level, and general math classes were dropped one full grade level. During the 2004–05 and 2005–06 school years, we offered three sections of algebra, one section of geometry, and one section of prealgebra at the eighth-grade level. During the same two-year period, the seventh-grade math curriculum consisted of one section of algebra and four sections of prealgebra.

In response to this major curriculum change in math, we also dropped all of our general math textbooks one grade level. Consequently, in grade levels for which a general math class still exists (fifth and sixth grades), students are working from a textbook that is one level higher than their grade-level placement. The fifth-grade students are using the old sixth-grade general math book, and the sixth-grade students are using the old seventh-grade text. Some curricular gaps needed to be covered in order for this transition to flow seamlessly, but all of the middle school math teachers made the necessary adjustments so that their students would be studying in more appropriate and challenging math classes.

Recently, I collected standardized test data to evaluate the effectiveness of this program change. Figure 4.1 reports the average growth that students in the sixth and eighth grades demonstrated on the Northwest Evaluation Association's MAP assessment for math.

Figure 4.1. MAP Assessment Test Results: Average Student Growth in Math

Year	Sixth Grade	Eighth Grade
(Fall to Spring Growth)		
2000–2001	5.34	3.19
2001–2002	6.11	4.59
2002–2003	7.98	5.77
2003–2004	9.66	4.35
2004–2005	8.35	5.87
2005–2006	8.9	4.0
(Fall to Fall Growth)		
2000–2001	8.65	5.03
2001–2002	6.99	4.98
2002–2003	5.66	2.98
2003–2004	11.14	2.72
2004–2005	9.51	7.34
2005–2006	8.0	7.9

As the data in Figure 4.1 indicate, the changes that we made to our math curriculum are paying dividends. To set the stage, it is important to understand what the average growth for a sixth-grade student is for the MAP assessment in math. The average growth of a sixth-grade student in math from fall to spring (same academic year) is 7.7 points. The first year (2003–04), when we moved the general seventh-grade math book to the sixth grade, our students demonstrated a mean growth (based on fall-to-spring testing) of 9.66 points on an equal interval RIT (Rasch Unit) scale—almost two full points higher than the norm group. Even more astounding is the 11.14-point average growth shown by the same group of students from fall to fall (which includes a summer off) during the 2003–04 school year, compared to the norm group's mean growth of 7.9 points—more than a three-point difference. Not only did those students demonstrate tremendous growth, but also they retained what they learned over the summer.

Another success attributable to our use of data translation came in March 2006. A student who would not have been selected for algebra as an eighth-grade student under the old criteria—whereby the seventh-grade teacher recommended only those students who had received a letter grade of A in every quarter and did not miss any assignments—did qualify under the data-driven criteria when he began the eighth grade. Now, as an eleventh grader, this student has qualified to take the American Invitational Math Exam, a privilege afforded to only the highest-performing juniors and seniors in math in America. Had we not changed the way we place students into math classes four years ago, who knows where this student would be today. Is it conceivable that this student, had he not been challenged in the eighth grade, might have become an even more severe discipline problem and perhaps even a high school dropout? I believe it is. However, because of we used data to make curriculum changes and because we challenged this student in spite of his less than stellar academic grades and homework record, he discovered four years ago that he was actually good at math and has performed even beyond his beliefs.

Another sweeping change that took place in my district as a result of using data to enhance student achievement was the design and implementation of a new remedial math program. As I mentioned, we use the MAP assessments quite extensively in our district. We administer those tests twice a year—once in the fall and once in the spring—to all students in grades 2–10 grade in the academic areas of reading, language usage, math, and science. A couple of years ago, after four years of administering the MAP assessments, I started to notice a trend in our elementary school. Our students were consistently scoring low in the area of number operations and relations. Even after bringing that information to the attention of the classroom teachers and urging that we needed to stress that area, our scores there were still not improving. Finally, we took the plunge at the elementary school and designed a remedial math program that we call Math Matters.

Students are placed in the program based on their test scores, academic performance in the classroom, and classroom teacher's recommendation. Our district math specialist teaches the Math Matters students. She is very knowledgeable about the MAP data and focuses her instruction strictly on the data. If, for example, she has four students who are scoring at about the same level in geometry, she will work with them all at the same time, regardless of their assigned grade level. She could have a first grader, a second grader, and two third-grade students working with her at the same time if their scores are in the same range. Once she gets them up to the appropriate grade level, she dismisses them. The Math Matters class is supplemental and does not take the place of the student's regular math instruction. Since the program was launched, the number operations and relations strand of the MAP assessment in math is no longer a weakness for us. More importantly, during the 2003–04 school year, 100% of the students serviced as third graders in the Math Matters program who were dismissed at the end of the year because they were performing at grade level scored at the proficient or advanced level on the state assessment as fourth-grade students in the fall of 2004. That is a *huge* success story for us!

The Math Matters program was expanded in January 2004. The district math specialist position was upgraded from a part-time position to a full-time position, and the district was able to provide support services to more students. During the 2004–05 school year, the Math Matters program was able to expand its eligibility criteria to include any child that was performing below his or her grade-level mean on the MAP assessments. Prior to that change, students had to be performing at or below the 34th percentile on the MAP assessments. The expansion of the program indicates that the achievement gap is closing, as the lowest-performing students are not as low as they were before the program was implemented. They are moving back into their grade-level math classes and seeing success. If more students can be serviced at higher levels, fewer students will be performing at the very low levels. In other words, our lowest-performing students are performing higher than they were in the past. According to the elementary school principal, "The Math Matters program has made a huge impact on our students at our school. What used to be identified as weaknesses on assessments are no longer present. We still have some work to do, but we are well on our way."

A third example of data translation in our district was the implementation of a middle school reading program that was entirely based on data. We made reading a required course for all middle school students beginning in the fall of 1998. Reading had been a required course for fifth- and sixth-grade students; however, seventh- and eighth-grade students were not required to take a reading course. After reviewing data and determining a need for such a course, we designed and implemented a required reading program for seventh- and eighth-grade middle school students. The MAP data identified a drop in reading scores related to the analysis of text and the application of reading strategies. Interestingly, the reading strategies scores dropped significantly when the students were no longer in a reading class. We hypothesized that if a required reading course was added for students in the seventh and eighth grades, the reading scores for that strand would improve, and reading scores would rise overall. It worked, and for its efforts to improve reading instruction for all students in the building, the middle school received the International Reading Association's Exemplary Reading Program Award in 2004.

According to the February/March 2005 issue of *Reading Today* magazine,

> This middle school is one of the few middle schools in Wisconsin to have required reading courses, in addition to a language arts class, for all four years of a students' middle-level education. The school added those courses about seven years ago as a way to improve the reading achievement at the middle level. The program is working. In the 2002–03 Wisconsin assessment, 97% of the districts' 113 eighth graders scored at the advanced or proficient level for the core subject area of reading. The remaining 3% scored at the basic level; none scored at the minimal performance level. For language arts, 86% scored at the advanced or proficient level. "The national trend in reading indicates a continual drop in reading performance from elementary school to middle school to high school," said the Director of Curriculum and Instruction/District Assessment Coordinator in the award application statement. "We are trying to break that cycle. We want our reading scores to continually improve as cohort groups pass through our facilities."

Translating district data into systemic change takes time and planning. Typical bandwagon approaches to writing curriculum and adopting new textbooks become much more focused efforts throughout the district. These examples indicate the power of analyzing and interpreting data to foster curricular and program changes in this school district. The data determine the need for change and help design what that change is. Implementing the DDIS model in a school district involves much more than collecting data and placing it into a warehouse for easy access. The data must be reviewed and translated into instructional change, or else it is simply more data.

Meticulous and calculated planning occurs in my district to translate data into systemic change, such as curriculum revision, content revision, and instructional adjustments. Teachers and administrators use their own data to create the "big picture" and to determine what adjustments need to be made.

The school district supports these initiatives with all of the resources that are possible, including new staff and new courses. The school board demands that every proposal that comes before them be fully researched and based on data. If the administrators can show a need for a program, course, or new teacher, the school board will support that decision with every resource at its disposal.

Data translation is the component of the DDIS model that involves content, curriculum, and program revision. What needs to be implemented and how it will be implemented are key planning tools related to actions in this component. Whatever changes are implemented must be planned, with implementation plans, guidelines, and purpose. Everyone involved must understand not only why something is being done but also how it will be done. I must caution, however, that this is also the component of the model that tends to spiral out of control if not monitored closely. The data translation component of the DDIS model must be the piece that moves school districts away from trying to do too many things. More than one districtwide initiative in a school district is too many. The focus must always be and forever remain on the data. What do the data suggest we need to do? How do the data suggest we do it? Staying focused during data translation is critical. Trying to do too many things at the same time will cause confusion and a loss of focus.

5

Data-Driven Instructional Design

How and When Are Data Translated Into Instructional Change at the Classroom Level?

What is really going on in the classroom based on data? Getting data to the classroom level so that it can be used by teachers to improve the instruction in their classrooms is the goal of this entire initiative and the heart of this book. If teachers do not have access to the data or if they are not using the data they have access to, this initiative will not be successful at improving student achievement. Moving the use of data to the classroom level is the biggest challenge in the Data-Driven Instructional System (DDIS) because it requires multiple components of the model to work together. For those components to work together seamlessly, structures must be in place for each and every component. For example, having a wonderful data-collection component is not very helpful if nothing is done with the data that are collected. Reflecting on data is busywork if no curriculum revision, content revision, or instructional changes result from it. Translating data at the program level into additional courses or staff will be somewhat effective, but moving the data to the classroom level is the key to changing the success of this data-driven initiative. When teachers are using data in their classrooms to meet the needs of every student, the data-driven initiative is well on its way to success.

The challenge of this system is to take large enough steps to keep moving forward as a district but small enough steps so that teachers do not become overwhelmed and rebellious. Getting the data into the hands of teachers so it can be used to mold classroom instruction is the broad goal of any data-driven initiative. What matters most is what is happening in the classroom—where the real learning takes place. Implementing the DDIS model for school improvement is impossible if teachers are not willing to use the data to change their instruction. Teachers need to own the data on their students. They need to work with the information and make it their own. They need to understand it and do something with it. All of that takes time and training, but it can be done. Once teachers see the value of using data to drive instruction and understand the purpose behind the initiative, they will experience those "aha!" moments when everything starts to make sense. Once that epiphany occurs, teachers will become the biggest enthusiasts of the data-driven initiative. Their attitude and desire for data to make decisions and affect the teaching and learning in their classroom will become infectious. At that moment, the data-driven initiative becomes a part of the everyday culture of a school district.

A middle school math teacher in the Barkdale School District commented, "It is important to identify the strengths and weaknesses of my students and go from there. How did they do on the test and where do I need to take them? What's the journey going to be as a result of this test? Once I know that and change my instruction to meet that, then I have come to the critical turning point with my instruction in my opinion." Clearly, this teacher has embraced the use of data in her classroom in order to change the instruction she delivers and to influence the learning of all students who enter and exit her classroom.

Another example comes from the Barkdale School District's reading specialist, who openly admitted that much of her time is spent at the elementary level—because that is where kids are learning to read. The district reading specialist worked with the kindergarten students and staff in the fall and made a discovery through the use of data.

She noted,

> The kindergarten teachers took a look at the data they have this year and determined they needed to do something more with vocabulary. Vocabulary really came out as a clear weakness in the data. It wasn't so much that students lacked vocabulary exposure, but they lacked the facility to interchange one vocabulary word for another. So there was great discussion about that and what could be done. The kindergarten teachers determined, as a result of their analysis that they were going to implement activities that forced kids to replace words. For example, the vocabulary word was *predator* so the kids had to come up with four or five other words that could be used in the same sentence as predator that would mean the same thing.

A third example of using data to drive instructional design comes from a high school classroom in Barkdale. One high school math teacher reported,

> We did an item analysis of our tenth-grade WKCE [Wisconsin Knowledge and Contents Exam]. One thing we noticed was that the students were weak in the questions that had to do with scale drawings which would be ratios and proportions. So in algebra

when we did ratios and proportions, we put in some exercises that involved doing scale drawings. We also made sure we were covering those things in our other math classes so the students who were not enrolled in algebra or geometry still got the practice they needed regarding scaled drawings.

A curriculum change in middle school math marked the fourth recognizable change based on data in the Barkdale School District. One teacher declared, "We were doing so poorly in math two years ago that we put together a math improvement team. Within a year we made some major changes to align curriculum as well as institute things like pacing charts and instructional strategies across the board. In certain instances it has made an instant impact on that curriculum review, at other times it is part of an ongoing process."

My district can point to similar examples that bring to life the use of data to change instructional practices at the classroom level. Several teachers in my district shared how they are using data in their classrooms to enhance student achievement. One high school math teacher said,

> I pour over the data to find specific high points and low points for specific students because I want to address their needs. If I see a class in which everybody does reasonably well with measurement and I'm teaching geometry, then I may not need to emphasize measurement as much. This changes how lessons are planned and how we do specific things.

A high school English teacher used her data in conjunction with early release days to plan tiered lessons for the students in her English classes. She also served on the District Leadership Team and used what she learned at the Data Retreats to change the instruction in her classroom.

> The most valuable thing for me is seeing the breakdown of how my students scored. They can say that someone is minimal but until I see and understand exactly what that means, it doesn't mean much to me. Something that dawned on me last year was that my students were having a horrible time picking the *best* answer to a multiple choice test question on that state test. There were two answers that could have been correct, but one of them was clearly the *best* answer. I saw a whole bunch of my sophomores just really bomb that. I remember thinking at the time that we needed to work on this. So, now if we read a short story, I will occasionally throw in a multiple choice question for my students and tell them to pick the *best* answer. We talk about the question and how a couple of the answer choices could be correct, but clearly one is better than the

other. That way, when they are asked to do this on a state test, they at least have some experience with it.

At the middle school level, an eighth-grade reading teacher used the data in her classroom to develop a vocabulary unit for her students. Interestingly, her students were well aware of the reason why they were working on their vocabulary because she has talked candidly with them about their Measures of Academic Progress (MAP) assessment data. Vocabulary had been identified as an area of weakness for her classes, so she told all of her classes that they would be working to improve their word analysis and vocabulary skills.

In this reading teacher's classroom, the students were the ones using data:

> We do a first-semester portfolio and a second-semester portfolio. Both semesters, the kids have to save all of their assignments from reading and language classes. They are provided with a list of the Wisconsin Model Academic Standards that they should have mastered for first semester and second semester. The students themselves have to actually correlate their assignments with the state standards and explain in writing how they think they have mastered each standard. I do simplify the language of the standards a little bit for them, but they are very familiar with the standards and the expectations of mastery. They are well aware of their learning as it relates to those standards. They understand why we did the assignments we did and it makes them think metacognitively about their own accomplishments. They are old enough to understand that they have some accountability too when it comes to their own learning.

A middle school special education teacher in our district used data to assist him with the development of Individualized Education Plans (IEPs) for his students. He relies on communications from the middle school staff for data that on the children he services in his special education program. This special education teacher services students at all grade levels in the middle school. He meets with all of the teachers at every grade level at least once a week to discuss the needs of his students. He used the assessment data in particular to provide intense instructional support where it was needed. He also felt that he came better prepared to IEP meetings when he had data to support his efforts in the classroom. He follows through with any grade-level initiatives brought forth through the data when he is working independently with his students. If he knows his eighth-grade students are working on vocabulary in reading class, he can reinforce that work with his students in his classroom.

The K–12 reading specialist in my district used data in the classroom in a multitude of ways. First, she had access to all of the district data, not just data on the students with whom she works. One of her responsibilities is to serve as a resource to all other staff members in the area of reading. When she was reviewing data after the spring 2004 MAP assessments, she realized that the mean scores were dropping in the measured objective goal area of analyzing text and applying reading strategies at the fifth-and sixth-grade levels. The K–12 district reading specialist is also a member of the District Leadership Team and brought up this discovery to the team during the summer 2004 Data Retreat. As a result, fifth- and sixth-grade students are now receiving the support services they need to improve their reading skills. Individual students have been identified through the use of MAP assessment data, classroom performance, and teacher recommendation. The district reading specialist facilitates a remedial reading group called "SOAR to Success" for these middle school students. Because no staff members were available to take on this additional remedial reading program, she had to do it. Although this commitment limits the time that she can spend helping classroom teachers with their reading instruction, it was a service that was clearly lacking in the middle school, and she filled the immediate need. The following year, I used the same data to recommend the addition of a staff person in reading support to the school board. That recommendation has since been filled with a full-time reading teacher who provides reading support to all of our middle school students. This staff addition is proof that the use of data not only changes classroom instruction but also provide evidence when additional staff are requested.

A second use of data by the district reading specialist encompassed much more of her title role. She decided to conduct a mini–Data Retreat for all of the third-grade teachers. This Data Retreat (Version 2, as it came to be known) focused all of the third-grade teachers' attention on the third-grade test given in Wisconsin to assess reading comprehension. The official name of this state assessment is the Wisconsin Reading Comprehension Test—An Assessment of Primary-Level Reading at Grade 3, but it is commonly referred to as the WRCT. The district reading specialist walked all of the third-grade teachers through the same process that the District Leadership Team goes through at a Data Retreat. The only difference was the length of the retreat and the assessment analyzed. The third-grade Data Retreat was one day in length, and the only assessment data discussed were related to the WRCT. The MAP assessment data and the WKCE data were never reviewed because they are typically the focus of the district Data Retreat. At the end of the one-day workshop, the third-grade teachers left with an action plan—based on data—that they used in their classrooms to improve reading comprehension.

The math specialist in my district explained that her whole program is based on data. In fact, her program exists *because* of data.

> My job is to identify students for my Math Matters program who are at risk and struggling in math or who are at risk for not mastering concepts. After I have identified students, I take those students in small groups because kids tend to learn well cooperatively and in a small group. My groups are small enough that the kids can help each other learn and I can give them focused instruction. I meet with the kids two or three days a week for one-half hour trying to focus on the deficits and bring them up to grade level so that they can succeed in the regular classroom. Who and what I teach all comes from the data. If students need to work on mathematical processes, that's what we work on. If they need to work on algebraic relationships, that's what we work on. My program is tailored to the individual needs of students based on data.

The district reading specialist worked cooperatively with one of the middle school teachers and helped her develop a differentiated lesson using the newspaper. She said, "We looked directly at the data to determine the need for sequencing with that group of students. Then we looked at what hands-on activity would be a good one that would show this sequencing. It was using the data to come up with a differentiated lesson for a classroom teacher."

The 1930s, the Dust Bowl, and a soup kitchen all come to life in my district as the middle school principal and the elementary school principal serve students their broth—an example of a data-driven instructional unit. Data suggested to a seventh-grade team of teachers that students did not truly understand concepts related to the 1930s. Discussions lead to the development on an integrated unit that brought together the academic areas of reading, language arts, and social studies in the seventh grade. The reading portion allows students to read one of three books that deal with the 1930s. The book that each student reads for this unit depends on data that identify his or her reading level. Those who need a lower-level book are given one (*Esperanza Rising*). Those who can excel are given a book that is at their level (*The Grapes of Wrath*). The average readers are given a book that challenges their thinking as well (*Out of the Dust*). Audio tapes were even ordered for two of the books to meet the needs of non-English-speaking students, and a Braille copy was ordered for a student who is blind. The reading assignments may vary, but the concepts that the students are expected to master by the end of the unit remain the same. The unit was developed based on data, and it uses data throughout the unit to meet the needs of individual students in the classroom.

The elementary principal summarized the use of data to drive instruction in the classrooms in his building by stating that his school now had teachers working with data and looking at the strengths and weaknesses of their students. He has seen this practice come to fruition through his classroom observations of instruction. The expectation is that teachers will take the data back to their classrooms to help them plan instruction and continue to fill in the gaps. Constant focus and follow-up ensure that this is, in fact, what is taking place. As the examples from the staff in my district indicate, teachers are using data to drive the instructional process in their classrooms—not just because they have to, but because they want to. They know what is best for the students in their district. The use of data really gets to the individual level of the students, meets them where they are, and moves them forward.

Whether the use of data to change instructional practices and to enhance student learning has effects that are systemic and formal or ongoing and informal is not the issue. What is important is that the instruction in the classroom is adjusted based on data to meet the individual needs of all students. All four of the examples given here indicate that change took place inside classrooms in two school districts. The changes made were based on data that was reviewed and translated into curriculum or classroom instructional changes. For data translation to move to data-driven instructional design in the DDIS model, school districts must get the data into the hands of classroom teachers so they can use it to improve instruction in their classrooms and meet the individual needs of the students they face every day. The examples shared in this chapter clearly illustrate the use of data at the classroom level.

6

Design Feedback

How and When Is the DDIS Model Adjusted and Evaluated for Success, and How Is Information Shared With School District Stakeholders?

Design feedback is the component of the Data-Driven Instructional System (DDIS) model that allows district officials to adjust current or ongoing initiatives based on results and to evaluate how information is being shared with the stakeholders in the school district, including students, parents, teachers, administrators, school board members, and the community. In both the Barkdale School District and my school district, students are given reports that provide feedback (like report cards), progress reports, and assessment results when they are taken. Parents, teachers, administrators, school board members, and the community all receive feedback on district performance and initiatives in a variety of ways.

In the Barkdale School District, the school improvement plans created at the summer Data Retreats are shared with all staff at the beginning of the school year so that everyone has a clear understanding of the district's and building's goals, and action plans are developed to achieve those goals. One high school English teacher gave an example of how the school improvement plan is shared with the full staff:

> We try to come up with two or three good, solid achievable goals at the Data Retreat every summer. Then at the start of the school year we always have those professional learning days. Those of us who attended the Data Retreat try and give the teachers that weren't there a mini-version of what we learned and explain that these are the goals we set. Then, as a group we start brainstorming ideas as to how we can go about reaching this goal. We have some ideas set, but everyone brainstorms some more about reaching the goals. We try and keep that focus throughout the school year and bring it back in front during professional learning opportunities and meetings throughout the school year. Are we always 100% focused? No we are not. But, that's what we try and do.

Teachers and administrators in my district operate with a similar approach to the sharing of information analyzed and interpreted at the summer

Data Retreat. The District Leadership Team identifies the major areas that are in need of improvement, such as reading, math, or science. The members of the District Leadership Team bring that information back to all of the members of their curricular department. In our district, every teacher is a member of a curricular department. Every grade level at the elementary school is represented in all of the four core academic area departments: English and language arts, mathematics, science, and social studies. The curricular department then determines how those major areas of need will be addressed in each building. SMART goals—strategic, measurable, attainable, results-oriented, and time-bound—related to the identified areas of need are written by every teacher in every building.

The teachers who work in exploratory or elective departments—physical education, music, art, family and consumer education, vocational education, business, and special education—are allowed to choose the area (reading or math) for which they want to write their SMART goal. They select the subject area that best relates to their content area. For example, the music department selected math because the teachers felt they could work on fractions when teaching whole notes, half notes, and quarter notes. The art department also selected math because those teachers felt they could emphasize the geometry strands of our Wisconsin math standards in their art classes when they talked about shapes, shading, and geometric design. The physical education teachers decided to focus on reading and have added components to their curriculum in which students read articles about current physical and mental health issues and wrote summaries of what they had read. Clearly, the district focus is on reading and math across grade levels and across curricular areas.

Throughout the school year, all teachers collect and analyze data related to their SMART goals and report back to their department heads. The department heads, in turn, report back to the District Leadership Team. As the District Leadership Team analyzes and interprets the departments' SMART goals, necessary adjustments are made to the school improvement plans at each school building. This cycle continues throughout the school year and provides the starting point for the summer Data Retreat. In addition to the data that the department heads share with the District Leadership Team, data are shared with the board of education formally twice a year at Academic School Board Retreats and informally once a month at regularly scheduled board of education meetings. The data shared at the board of education meetings are also reported in the newspaper to all public constituents, including parents, students, and community members, as the local press covers every meeting.

In the Barkdale School District, teachers also use design feedback when they talk with each other and discuss their interpretation of the assessment data. The Measures of Academic Progress (MAP) data are not directly published in the local newspaper or shared with the community. Only the results of the interpretation of the MAP data are reported—for example, the implementation of a new program based on data, the creation of a new instructional position and the hiring of that position, or the progress of a school improvement plan. Data from the Wisconsin Knowledge and Content (WKCE) exam—that is, the actual percentages of students at each performance level—are publicized in the local newspaper for all to see, and they are often compared with the results in surrounding districts. Employees of the school district must be prepared to answer any questions that may arise from the publicized performance data. Barkdale's district administrator stated, "We use the results of the MAP testing and take a look at that at a meeting with all administrators and teachers by grade level to see where things are going. Have we been successful in what we set out to do? And, of course, there is always discussion around WKCE when that information comes out. Teachers want to see the results." In Wisconsin, the WKCE assessment results are always published in the local newspaper, and teachers and administrators need to answer to the public for those scores.

In addition to the local newspaper, parents and community members in Barkdale are kept abreast of the school district's progress through public meetings, the district newsletter, and the school district's cable news channel. Furthermore, parents receive report cards and assessment reports at the end of each quarter or after the administration of an assessment. The director of curriculum and instruction for the Barkdale School District also writes regular informative articles for the local newspaper that help parents understand the data they are receiving at home and explain how they can and should interpret that data. More recently, an Internet portal was established in the Barkdale School District so that parents of children enrolled in any of the Barkdale schools can have immediate access to information on their children.

The school board receives feedback at board meetings through administrative reports. Each month, all building-level administrators are required to provide a brief report on their respective building. The director of curriculum and instruction is also required to report to the school board monthly on district-level data and information. The influence of the work of Richard DuFour and his professional learning communities philosophy was clear when I spoke with the principal at Barkdale Elementary and Middle School. He said it best when he summarized the design feedback in his district:

> You know—this isn't rocket science. We focus on three things: What do we want students to learn, how will we know if they've learned it, and what are we going to do if they haven't learned it? From there, you have two avenues—is it the curriculum or the instruction that is causing some children to not understand? Once

that is determined, something must be done to remedy the situation.

Design feedback comes in many forms in the Barkdale School District. Teachers give feedback to students and parents, building-level administrators give feedback to teachers, district-level administrators give feedback to building-level administrators and teachers, parents give feedback to district- and building-level administrators and teachers, and district- and building-level administrators give feedback to the school board and the community. Barkdale School District is constantly evaluating what it is doing and whether it is successful. If it finds the district is not succeeding at something it set out to do, it adjusts and tries to improve the situation from another angle. This is truly an ongoing process in Barkdale, as the district administrator stated earlier.

The teachers and administrators in my district are constantly reflecting on the job they are doing. Every Wednesday, we have an after-school meeting of some sort: the first Wednesday is a staff meeting, the second Wednesday is a grade-level meeting, the third Wednesday is a K–12 department meeting, and the fourth Wednesday is a reading or math meeting. The District Leadership Team also meets on a regular basis to assess the progress of the school improvement plan. They talk about what is working, what is not working, and how they can adjust and improve the plan for the remainder of the year.

Monthly staff meetings center not only on managerial tasks that need to be completed but also the sharing of classroom activities that work. Sharing best practices is a part of every staff meeting in every building in the district. Building principals are responsible for including discussion of the school improvement plan at the building level and reporting progress made toward the goals during building staff meetings.

At grade-level meetings (elementary school) or during team time (middle school), progress toward the school improvement goals is discussed as it relates to each grade level. Data on students are discussed, and plans for improvement are developed. Grade levels and teams send out electronic summaries of their meetings to all staff members and district-level specialists on a daily basis. As the director of curriculum and instruction, the district assessment coordinator, and the district data manager, I receive summaries from every grade level every single day. The district reading specialist, the guidance counselors, the district math specialist, and the Title I reading teachers also receive the electronic summaries from every grade level on a daily basis.

K–12 department meetings are strategically planned by the department heads under administrative direction to ensure a continued focus on students' progress toward the achievement goals set forth during the summer

Data Retreat. Again, the focus remains on the data and progress toward goals. Other departmental tasks (such as budgeting and textbook selection) are handled at K–12 department meetings, but most of the time is spent reflecting on student performance in the subject area and the goals that the department has set for itself.

Because reading and math have been the focus in our district for several years, we set aside one Wednesday per month for either a reading or a math meeting. These meetings involve not just reading and math teachers but everyone in grades K–8. The school improvement plans are focused on improving performance in reading and math, so providing all teachers with time to discuss data related to these two subject areas is a necessity in my district. For example, one of the goals at the middle school level is to improve the performance of reading through the use of content reading strategies. Because this goal encompasses all curricular areas, everyone is involved in the meetings. The district reading specialist uses this time to demonstrate reading strategies in several curricular areas so that all teachers understand that they are all teachers of reading. Providing the instructional staff with professional learning on the use of reading strategies in their content area gives them the confidence they need to implement the reading strategies in their classrooms. The monthly math meetings have given us an opportunity to accomplish two major initiatives in the math area: (1) We streamlined our curriculum to create emphasis areas at every grade level, and (2) time was set aside to analyze our MAP data related to math. This time allows us to determine which curricular areas at each grade level need improvement so that we can teach those areas first. This ensures that our weakest areas are addressed first and for as long as it takes for students to demonstrate mastery.

Outside the school walls, parents are provided with report cards at the end of every marking period during the school year. Parents of children attending either the elementary or middle school in our district also receive progress reports every three weeks during a single marking period. The parents of children in high school receive a progress report every fourth week of any marking period. State assessment data from the WKCE are sent home to parents of children in grades that are tested. MAP assessment reports are sent home to parents twice a year after the administration of the assessments. Along with the assessment report, a letter from the director of curriculum and instruction explains how to interpret the report, and statistical information is include to give parents an sense of how their child should be performing.

Parents, community members, school board members, teachers, and students all stay informed by reading the newspaper in our district, as in Barkdale. My district is home to two local newspapers, so there are ample opportunities to have school events and happenings covered in the local press.

Our Web site provides parents, community members, students, and staff with pertinent information and recent press releases from the school district.

School board members are given feedback in a variety of ways. All administrators in the district are required to give a monthly report at every school board meeting. Principals report on the events and progress in their buildings, while district-level administrators report on the progress of the district. Twice a year, the school board attends an Academic School Board Retreat with the administrators. This retreat provides administrators with an opportunity to communicate school improvement progress in their buildings or at the district level to the school board members in a concentrated fashion. It is not conducted as a typical board meeting but is an additional meeting that was implemented for the sole purpose of informing the school board. During the 2004–05 school year, an additional academic retreat was added for school board members and administrators. Teachers working in support roles in the district conducted this informational academic retreat in December of 2004. The purpose of this academic retreat was for members of the school board to hear and understand exactly what these support people do and how they affect the educational system in the district.

Communication with the school board is an essential part of design feedback. We have found that having a summer Data Retreat with the District Leadership Team, followed by an Academic School Board Retreat in December to update the school board on the progress of the school improvement plans and then another in the spring, is an effective way to keep all school board members informed.

The most recent endeavor related to the design feedback component of the DDIS model in my district was the implementation of Parent Connect. Parent Connect is a module of our Student Information System (available from NCS Pearson) that gives parents an Internet portal they can use to check the grades, attendance, or assignments of their children. The implementation of this software program gives parents of students enrolled in the district a direct link to data on their children. Each family has its own user name and password and can only view the data on their students. Parents are aware of everything from attendance and grades to the balance in their lunch account.

Design feedback should not be construed as a component that is stagnant or that occurs only after the data-driven instructional design component. Design feedback is a component of the DDIS model that forces schools and school districts to constantly evaluate what they are doing and whether it is making a difference. Design feedback is occurring all the time in a district that is functioning under a data-driven instructional philosophy.

7

Summative and Formative Assessment

What Types of Assessment Data Are Most Useful for Informing Instruction?

There are two basic types of assessments: summative and formative. Each type of assessment has a distinct purpose and is used for different reasons. Summative assessments are typically given at the end of a unit or lesson to determine whether a student has mastered a concept or the degree to which he or she has understood the lesson. State assessments to meet the requirements of the No Child Left Behind (NCLB) Act are considered summative because they are given once a year and are used to determine whether students meet state-determined criteria. Summative assessments are not given very often and typically are not used to inform instructional decisions; rather, they are used to determine whether learning has actually taken place. They are considered the culminating experience of instruction. Formative assessments, on the other hand, are used more often to determine strengths and weaknesses of a student's understanding. They are used to diagnose student learning needs before, during, and after instruction takes place. Formative assessments provide teachers and students with information that can be used to tailor instructional efforts based on need.

Working in a culture in which formative assessments are used to determine how and when a topic should be taught to students takes some getting used to. Teachers have traditionally used assessments in a much more summative way to determine whether their students have mastered the concepts they have just taught. There are still classrooms across America that look the same every September—meaning that the teachers are teaching the same things, using the same resources, with the same lesson plans. The problem with this approach is that every September, the students in those classrooms are different. There is an old saying that states, "If you always do what you've always done, you'll always get what you've always gotten." In this age of educational accountability, what we have always gotten is not good enough. Something must change if schools and districts are to avoid being identified as in need of improvement under the NCLB legislation. In order to achieve different results, we must do something differently. What can be changed in schools? One thing remains constant—the students are different every year in every classroom, yet schools and districts are held to the same standards. Regardless of the abilities of the children in front of a teacher in any given year, those students have to perform, and it is up to the teacher to make that happen. It is the responsibility of school district leaders to provide teachers with every possible tool to assist them and their students on their journey toward success.

Viewing assessment in a different light may be difficult for some. Originally, assessment was used to determine whether a person had mastered a particular concept or lesson. Historically, standardized assessments were given to find out whether a school district met the requirements to continue receiving federal funding. Traditionally, assessments were given at the end of a unit or chapter to measure what students had learned using the assessment as a summative tool. If teachers found after the summative assessment that students had not fully mastered the concepts taught, the teacher recorded the grade the student received on the assessment and moved on with the planned instruction, encouraging the low-performing student to work harder the next time.

One of the keys to the success of the Data-Driven Instructional System (DDIS) is changing our perceptions of assessment. Whether summative or formative, each type of assessment has a purpose. Determining the purpose of an assessment and sharing that purpose with all stakeholders in a data-driven system is critical. Everyone must know why they are assessing: Is it to inform instruction or to determine whether students have "met the bar" set forth on a state or national assessment? The data from each type of assessment are used in very different ways.

According to Stiggins, Arter, Chappuis, and Chappuis (2004), all assessment falls into one of two general categories: assessments *for* learning and assessments *of* learning. "Both categories have their place in education and in the classroom—you've been doing both for years. What is perhaps new is an expanded understanding of the roles each should play to maximize student achievement while minimizing unintended negative consequences and side effects for students" (Stiggins et al., 2004, p. 29). Assessments of learning determine whether learning has, in fact, occurred. State assessments, local standardized tests, and college entrance exams are all examples of assessments of learning. Assessments for learning occur while learning is still taking place. Assessments that teachers conduct throughout teaching and learning to diagnose student needs, plan for instruction, and provide students with feedback that will help them guide their own learning experiences are examples of assessments for learning.

The Barkdale School District gives summative assessments at the end of a unit or chapter to check for mastery, but it also administers formative assessments. Formative assessments are not given at the end but rather the beginning of instruction, and they are used to inform the instructional process as it is occurring. The director of curriculum and instruction in Barkdale said, "The assessment is really the first stop at determining what we are going to be teaching our kids." This statement implies that the assessment must come before the instruction, and therefore it is formative in nature rather than summative. "In the past, I think the assessment was the outcome, yes. I still believe the knee-jerk reaction to look at the assessment as summative is there because that is what the state and federal governments publish. You know that is still going to be looked at, but we really try and not make that the focal point," the director of curriculum and instruction explained.

Another Barkdale administrator shared an example of a formative assessment used in his district. Based on the district's history of less than perfect math scores on the state exam, the Barkdale School District created a Math Improvement Team. This team decided that it needed to make some changes based on assessment data—not just the Wisconsin Knowledge and Concepts Exam data but also the Measures of Academic Progress (MAP) data. The middle school math teachers decided to use flexible groupings of students based on their math data results, pacing charts were added at all middle school levels, and curriculum changes were made. This Barkdale's middle school principal noted,

> Since we have been doing all those things, the teachers have been watching the MAP test results and seeing them get better and better. The kids' math scores are going up. I suppose we are going to reach a plateau at some level, or at some time, but that is one of the key indicators of success. We *do* look at those scores a little bit and wonder if the changes we made in math are the reason the kids math scores are going up. It could be. It certainly could be one of the factors.

According to one math teacher at Barkdale Middle School, using the assessment data to inform his instruction provided him with facts. "Well, let's put it this way, it's concrete. You know, we can go with a lot of abstract things, but this is concrete. It's right there in front of your nose." A Barkdale High School teacher viewed assessments in the same way, but did not feel they were being used quite so informatively at her level. "We need to do a better job of that. I would love to see us do more with that data. We all just seem like we already have so much on our plates that we don't find the time we should to look at and analyze the data to inform our instruction. I don't think we are doing a very good job with that at all at the high school—at least not in my department."

My district does administer standardized assessments that are summative in nature (state-mandated measures of accountability), but they have also moved beyond those assessments to implement other standardized assessments that are used in a formative way. The DDIS model requires school districts to see assessment in a whole new light. Under the guise of the DDIS model, assessments are given at the beginning of a unit or chapter of study to check what students already know—thus, the assessment is used in a formative way to guide instruction from that point forward. Assessments are the beginning of instruction rather than the end. Assessment is ongoing in the classroom during instruction and also takes place at the end of instruction to measure student growth. One high school English teacher stated,

> Since I came here, the state test scores have been very high and it's my understanding that they have been on a steady increase. I think that speaks to the fact, the awareness, that once teachers become more aware of what is going on and how to use the data, they can figure out what kids are having difficulties with as well as which kids need to be challenged. With the kids who are having difficulties, we can figure out exactly what areas we need to address in the curriculum and we see their scores blossom. Improvement all the way around is not just seen in test scores, but in everyday class work.

The shift from summative to formative assessment was not easy in the school district in which I work. Our transformation began in 1999. Prior to the implementation of the MAP assessment, we had only the state data on which to base decisions. We knew that we needed a better, more comprehensive tool to use for decision-making purposes, so we implemented the MAP assessments during the 1998–99 school year. Those tests are computer based and use branching technology, meaning that the test adjusts to the students' ability level. The MAP assessments are aligned with the Wisconsin Model Academic Standards, so we felt confident in selecting that assessment as our new tool.

The change did not come without resistance, however. The district administrator and I had to meet with every teacher and assure them that this assessment would not be used to evaluate their teaching. We implemented the assessment to improve instruction for kids—period. We've made mistakes along the way, but we have stayed the course, and it has proven to be the right thing for the students. We have implemented countless programs and changed the way instruction is conducted in classrooms throughout the district because we have given teachers the tools they need to truly make a difference.

Every step of this process was meticulously planned and calculated. Teachers were only given bits at a time. The first year, we gave the assessments. Then we began talking about the results of the assessments in the second year, still in a very summative way. We wanted to know whether our students had grown throughout the year. In the third year, we began to encourage teachers to plan lessons in their classrooms based on general data from the MAP assessments. Were their students high, average, or low? They needed to make some adjustments. Since then, we have implemented tiered lesson planning and differentiated instruction based on the strands of the assessments. We did not want to overwhelm teachers, but we needed things to change in order to improve. Of course, along the way, the most important thing is to provide training to the teachers. We cannot ask them to do things they have never done before or don't know how to do. If we did that, they would have gotten frustrated and given up. We took baby steps and went from the whole to the part. We are still refining the process. Every time teachers review data in our district and use it to change the instruction in their classrooms, they are getting better. The staff should be proud of their efforts thus far, and I believe they are. Now, they get excited about what they find in their data, and they immediately begin to think of ways to improve. We used to try to figure out why a particular student scored the way he or she did on a state assessment. Now, we look at the score and figure out how to change the system so that child can succeed. We have moved away from making excuses to focus on creating solutions. The change has been slow, but it has been the most rewarding experience of my educational career.

Using assessment as a formative tool rather than a summative tool has even helped one classroom teacher to call out her less motivated students: "Some of the kids that are testing really high would like me to believe that they are not so bright. I love when they do that and I call them on it right away," a high school teacher said. Some students believe they can pull the wool over their teacher's eyes, but when data exist to refute their claim, the students have no choice but to admit they were trying to get away with something.

The district math specialist, whose Math Matters program is fully designed using formative data, said,

> State assessments are based on state standards. Year after year we go back to our state standards to address the things that we need to teach and when we need to teach them. The standards are aligned to the test, so we are bound to do well on the state tests if we teach what the data say our kids need. I believe that teachers and school districts are wasting their time if they are taking a formative assess-

ment and not using the data from those assessments to make a difference in the classroom.

Teachers here are seeing their district transform right in front of their eyes. According to one high school math teacher, this data-driven initiative is something worth doing in any school district because it improves instruction.

> When you sit at our Data Retreat and you look at the interaction of the teachers and the administrators, everybody putting their heads together and saying these are the things we are doing right, these are the things we are doing wrong...and this is the data to support that...that communication is evidence enough for me that it's something other schools should be doing.

Two middle school teachers in our district spoke about the district's success and related that success to the high expectations of the students, staff, and administration. They explained that everyone involved in the educational process in this district believes they are responsible for the education of every child, and it shows in the ways they have adjusted their instruction by using assessments in a formative rather than summative way. The eighth-grade reading teacher thought back to the first full day of school this year and remembered a question from her principal:

> Our principal got up in front of us for our opening staff meeting and out of the blue asked us to raise our hand if we were a teacher of special education students. Every hand in the room went up from the art teacher to the science teachers—everyone—and it wasn't rehearsed. That speaks volumes to the culture in this district and our ability to succeed. Every person here takes the responsibility to teach every child. We do not look for reasons to exclude special students from our classrooms, but rather we search for ways to make them successful within our classrooms.

Using a data-driven system to enhance student achievement is clearly evident in the district in which I work. From the superintendent to the students, everyone realizes how important it is to use data in a formative way to inform instructional decisions and to really make a difference in the lives of students. Though the use of data in our classrooms still varies, the philosophy of the data-driven system seems to have permeated all of the concrete walls to reach the classrooms in all buildings. This district has gone beyond general curriculum changes and now aims to meet the needs of each and every individual student based on data.

In order for assessments to truly become formative tools that school districts can use to improve classroom instruction, teachers must focus their instruction on the individual needs of students through differentiation and tiered lesson planning. That way, all students receive the instruction they need, at the level they need it, and can progress from there. "We're used to thinking about assessment as the measurer of impact of instructional interventions; we implement a new program or teaching strategy and then use assessment to see how effective it was. In the case of assessment for learning, assessment becomes not only the measurer of impact, but also the innovation that causes change in student achievement; assessment is not just the index of change, it is the change" (Stiggins et al., 2004).

8

Summary and Results: Is It Worth It?

Implementing and using the Data-Driven Instructional System (DDIS) model requires due diligence and commitment on the part of the school district. There must be a person within the district who is willing to take on the role of "data champion" to keep the initiative moving forward. This chapter will summarize some of the results we have seen in my district, demonstrating that implementing the DDIS model for school improvement is definitely worth it.

Some of the results we have seen have been phenomenal. Since its inception, the DDIS model for school improvement has made a tremendous difference in the success of our students. Since the fall of 1999, our district has made several changes in the area of reading instruction based on data. For example, the elementary and middle schools in my district have implemented a Reading Recovery program and have brought in RSVP (Retired Senior Volunteer Person) readers, senior volunteers who come to school two or three times a week to read with a child. They have added a literacy support coordinator to coordinate family and community literacy activities with the school. A guided reading program in kindergarten and the first grade, which provides children with appropriate reading materials at their level, will be expanded to the second grade in 2006–07 and to the third grade in 2007–08. The Title I reading program, a remedial reading instruction for students in grades 1–7, has been expanded, and a required reading course has been added for all students through grade 8.

Figures 8.1 and 8.2 report reading data from the Wisconsin Knowledge and Concepts Exam (WKCE) over the last seven years and the mean reading score on the Northwest Evaluation Association's Measure of Academic Progress (MAP) assessments, which are given twice a year (fall and spring). Figure 8.1 reports the percentage of students who performed at the advanced or proficient level and those who performed at the minimal or basic level. Figure 8.1 is coded to show matched cohort group performance and to easily identify whether the same students improved as they progressed through the grade levels. Figure 8.2 displays the mean RIT score (Rasch Unit, an equal interval scale that ranges from 150 to 360 on the MAP assessments) in reading by grade level and testing term, as well as the mean growth in reading demonstrated each year by grade level.

From Figure 8.1, it is clear that the progress we are making in my district from the fourth to the eighth grade has been positive, whereas growth on this assessment from eighth to tenth grade has been less positive. My district, a mirror image of the national trend in reading, has seen a decline in reading performance between the eighth and tenth grade. However, looking only at the tenth-grade results, it is evident that students are performing better overall: The percentage of students scoring proficient or advanced has steadily increased over the last five years, with the exception of 2003–04. Looking at all of the data by grade level, huge gains can be identified between the 1999–2000 school year and the 2005–06 school year. In 1999–2000, the percentage of students scoring proficient or advanced in reading in the fourth grade was 89.55%. That same grade level now has 90.33% of students performing at the proficient or advanced level. The eighth-grade results went from 90.63% proficient or advanced during 1999–2000 to 94.13% during the 2005–06 school year. The performance of tenth-grade students in reading at the proficient or advanced level went from 82.88% during 1999–2000 to 90.67% during 2005–06.

These data clearly show an improvement in reading performance in my district since the 1999–2000 school year—the year we began to implement a DDIS model for school improvement.

Figure 8.1. Wisconsin Knowledge and Concepts Exam (WKCE) Reading Results

Grade	Performance Levels	1999-2000	2000-2001	2001-2002	2002-2003	2003-2004	2004-2005	2005-2006
3	Minimal and Basic							11.87%
	Proficient and Advanced	*This Grade Not Tested with WKCE During These Years*						88.13%
	All							100.00%
4	Minimal and Basic	7.46%	8.96%	12.79%	10.00%	15.87%	12.33%	9.67%
	Proficient and Advanced	89.55%	89.55%	84.88%	88.57%	84.13%	87.67%	90.33%
	All	100.00%	100.00%	100.00%	100.00%	100.00%	100.00%	100.00%
5	Minimal and Basic							13.87%
	Proficient and Advanced							86.13%
	All							100.00%
6	Minimal and Basic	*These Grades Not Tested with WKCE During These Years*						6.87%
	Proficient and Advanced							93.13%
	All							100.00%
7	Minimal and Basic							10.32%
	Proficient and Advanced							89.68%
	All							100.00%
8	Minimal and Basic	9.38%	8.41%	13.46%	2.68%	5.94%	6.67%	5.87%
	Proficient and Advanced	90.63%	91.59%	85.58%	97.32%	94.06%	93.33%	94.13%
	All	100.00%	100.00%	100.00%	100.00%	100.00%	100.00%	100.00%
10	Minimal and Basic	17.12%	12.98%	22.33%	16.22%	21.70%	13.22%	9.33%
	Proficient and Advanced	82.88%	87.02%	77.67%	83.78%	78.30%	86.78%	90.67%
	All	100.00%	100.00%	100.00%	100.00%	100.00%	100.00%	100.00%

Figure 8.2 displays the mean RIT score for reading by grade level on the Northwest Evaluation Association's MAP assessment. My district gives this assessment twice a year (fall and spring) in grades 2–10 in the subject areas of reading, language usage, math, and science. The mean growth by grade level for the last six years is highlighted in gray in Figure 8.2. Again, the mean growth increased in every grade level, with one exception, from 2000–01 through 2005–06. The scores of second-grade students grew 3.67 points during the 2000–01 school year, compared to 17.16 points during the 2005–06 school year. Some may suggest that the growth figures are going up because the overall scores are going down. However, that is not the case in my district. Even more interesting—and evidenced by the data—the mean scores are not going down. While growth is increasing, so are the mean scores by grade level. Thus, not only is the growth in scores increasing, but also the mean scores are increasing. This is a tremendous accomplishment: The fall scores from 2000–01 went up by approximately 5 points in every grade level by the 2005–06 school year. As any experienced educator will note, we are achieving these results with different students every year. Though some educators use this fact as an excuse to explain poor performance, it is clear that if teachers use the data they have and change the instruction in their classrooms accordingly, it does not matter which students are sitting in front of them.

Figure 8.2. Mean RIT Scores for Reading by Grade Level on the MAP Assessment

Grade	Term	2000–2001	2001–2002	2002–2003	2003–2004	2004–2005	2005–2006
2	Fall	179.4 (70)	176.49 (65)	173.37 (65)	177.87 (69)	176 (69)	177.82 (78)
	Spring	183.07 (70)	185.13 (65)	189.52 (65)	192.29 (69)	192.76 (69)	194.98 (78)
	Growth	3.67	8.64	16.15	14.42	16.76	17.16
3	Fall	195.27 (69)	189.14 (76)	189.33 (67)	191.49 (67)	193.88 (66)	191.33 (69)
	Spring	197.34 (88)	198.53 (76)	199.73 (67)	202.81 (67)	204 (66)	202.72 (69)
	Growth	2.07	9.39	10.4	11.32	10.12	11.39
4	Fall	205.7 (69)	199.45 (89)	198.38 (72)	197.8 (66)	202.18 (76)	201.42 (69)
	Spring	206.54 (69)	204.88 (89)	205.32 (72)	205.83 (66)	209.68 (76)	207.81 (69)
	Growth	0.84	5.43	6.94	8.03	7.5	6.39
5	Fall	206.71 (49)	205.96 (75)	205.36 (86)	206.45 (74)	205.57 (67)	206.29 (78)
	Spring	210.77 (49)	211.19 (75)	214.36 (86)	211.61 (74)	214.83 (67)	215.18 (78)
	Growth	4.06	5.23	9	5.16	9.26	8.89
6	Fall	215.3 (88)	213.58 (76)	209.6 (77)	211.2 (94)	213.01 (76)	213.13 (68)
	Spring	218.64 (88)	217.6 (76)	217.2 (77)	217.3 (94)	215.78 (76)	218.71 (68)
	Growth	3.34	4.02	3.62	6.1	2.77	5.58
7	Fall	217.96 (112)	220.48 (111)	218.06 (105)	215 (105)	218.57 (112)	218.59 (99)
	Spring	222.32 (112)	223.14 (111)	221.72 (105)	219.84 (105)	222.52 (112)	222.94 (99)
	Growth	4.36	2.66	3.66	4.84	3.95	4.35
8	Fall	226 (109)	221.18 (112)	224.48 (113)	223.41 (103)	221.56 (107)	224.85 (111)
	Spring	226.54 (109)	223.42 (112)	228.32 (113)	226.14 (103)	226.25 (107)	228.4 (111)
	Growth	0.54	2.24	3.84	2.73	4.69	3.55
9	Fall	225.81 (106)	226.25 (106)	225.53 (111)	227.35 (125)	225.38 (104)	226.59 (101)
	Spring	225.2 (106)	227.06 (106)	225.01 (111)	229.34 (125)	227.79 (104)	229.84 (101)
	Growth	-0.61	0.81	-0.52	1.99	2.41	3.25
10	Fall	229.54 (131)	226.58 (105)	229.48 (110)	225.67 (110)	228.77 (126)	229.32 (99)
	Spring	229.77 (131)	228.73 (105)	230.2 (110)	226.54 (110)	231.48 (126)	232.36 (99)
	Growth	0.23	2.15	0.72	0.87	2.71	3.04

Under the requirements of the No Child Left Behind Act, not only are school districts held accountable for the performance of all students as a group, but also they are held accountable for certain subgroups of students. Those subgroups include students with disabilities, students who speak limited English, students of a minority ethnicity, and students who are economically disadvantaged. Our district had been struggling to close an identifiable achievement gap between our regular education students (non-DIS) and our students with disabilities (DIS) until we began to use data to inform all instruction, including the instruction of students with disabilities. Recently, beginning with the 2004–05 school year, we began to service students with disabilities who were either identified with a learning disability or an emotional or behavioral disability through our Title I reading program if they also had an identified reading need. This concept came out of our district Data Retreat during the summer of 2004. The members of the District Leadership Team, who were also teachers of children with disabilities, suggested a change to our Title I program.

Figure 8.3 makes clear that the gap between students in special education programs and those in regular education programs has dramatically decreased over the last six years. The second-grade gap in reading achievement declined from 20.06 points in the fall of 2000 to 4.64 points in the spring of 2006. That is an incredible decrease that we fully attribute to our use of data to drive instructional practices in the classroom and our expansion of programs to provide assistance to students who would otherwise not receive such services. The reading gap in the third grade declined from 30.5 points in the fall of 2000 to 8 points in the spring of 2006; in the fourth grade, from 17.75 points in the fall of 2000 to 6.67 points in the spring of 2006; in the fifth grade, from 28.53 points in the fall of 2000 to 15.34 points in the spring of 2006; and in the sixth grade, from 15.68 points in the fall of 2000 to 12.09 points in the spring of 2006. In the seventh and ninth grade, the data show an increase in the achievement gap between the fall of 2000 and the spring of 2006, an exception that will be addressed during an upcoming Data Retreat. Overall, however, the reading achievement gap between nondisabled students and students with disabilities in my district has closed.

Figure 8.3. Northwest Evaluation Association's Mean Reading RIT Score on MAP Tests for Nondisabled and Disabled Students

Grade	Year	Term	MAP Score Non-EEN	MAP Score EEN	Gap
2	2000–2001 2000–2001	Fall Spring	181.69 (62) 187.27 (62)	161.63 (8) 158.64 (8)	20.06 28.63
	2001–2002 2001–2002	Fall Spring	178.82 (50) 187.81 (50)	168.73 (15) 175 (15)	10.09 12.81
	2002–2003 2002–2003	Fall Spring	175.44 (57) 190.98 (57)	158.63 (8) 180.56 (8)	16.81 10.42
	2003–2004 2003–2004	Fall Spring	179.23 (62) 193.36 (62)	165.86 (7) 183 (7)	13.37 10.36
	2004–2005 2004–2005	Fall Spring	177.32 (62) 194.78 (62)	164.29 (7) 176.88 (7)	13.03 17.9
	2005–2006 2005–2006	Fall Spring	178.48 (64) 195.72 (64)	174.54 (14) 191.08 (14)	3.94 4.64
3	2000–2001 2000–2001	Fall Spring	198.39 (79) 199.59 (79)	167.89 (9) 174.88 (9)	30.5 24.71
	2001–2002 2001–2002	Fall Spring	193.69 (62) 202.73 (62)	169 (14) 179.93 (14)	24.69 22.8
	2002–2003 2002–2003	Fall Spring	192.46 (54) 201.96 (54)	176.31 (13) 189 (13)	16.15 12.96
	2003–2004 2003–2004	Fall Spring	193.41 (58) 204.42 (58)	179.11 (9) 192.22 (9)	14.3 12.2
	2004–2005 2004–2005	Fall Spring	195.2 (55) 205.2 (55)	187.27 (11) 198.09 (11)	7.93 7.11
	2005–2006 2005–2006	Fall Spring	192.57 (58) 204 (58)	184.82 (11) 196 (11)	7.75 8
4	2000–2001 2000–2001	Fall Spring	207.75 (61) 208.31 (61)	190 (8) 193 (8)	17.75 15.31
	2001–2002 2001–2002	Fall Spring	203.64 (77) 207.71 (77)	172.58 (12) 183.4 (12)	31.06 24.31
	2002–2003 2002–2003	Fall Spring	201.57 (63) 208.82 (63)	176 (9) 182.6 (9)	25.57 26.22
	2003–2004 2003–2004	Fall Spring	201.41 (56) 208.5 (56)	177.6 (10) 189.78 (10)	23.81 18.72
	2004–2005 2004–2005	Fall Spring	204.09 (67) 210.85 (67)	188 (9) 199.75 (9)	16.09 11.1
	2005–2006 2005–2006	Fall Spring	203.61 (59) 209 (59)	192 (10) 202.33 (10)	11.61 6.67

NWEA Reading MAP Gap Analysis *Continued*

Grade	Year	Term	MAP Score Non-EEN	MAP Score EEN	Gap
5	2000–2001	Fall	213.7 (37)	185.17 (12)	28.53
	2000–2001	Spring	214.62 (37)	191.23 (12)	23.39
	2001–2002	Fall	208.66 (65)	188.4 (10)	20.26
	2001–2002	Spring	213.47 (65)	196.6 (10)	16.87
	2002–2003	Fall	209.07 (76)	177.2 (10)	31.87
	2002–2003	Spring	218.09 (76)	188.27 (10)	29.82
	2003–2004	Fall	207.94 (65)	195.67 (9)	12.27
	2003–2004	Spring	214.11 (65)	195.1 (9)	19.01
	2004–2005	Fall	207.61 (56)	197.45 (11)	10.16
	2004–2005	Spring	217.7 (56)	202.17 (11)	15.53
	2005–2006	Fall	207.77 (67)	195 (10)	12.77
	2005–2006	Spring	216.9 (67)	201.56 (10)	15.34
6	2000–2001	Fall	216.9 (79)	201.22 (9)	15.68
	2000–2001	Spring	219.9 (79)	205.75 (9)	14.15
	2001–2002	Fall	216.21 (66)	196.2 (10)	20.01
	2001–2002	Spring	219.93 (66)	201.3 (10)	18.63
	2002–2003	Fall	211.03 (71)	192.67 (6)	18.36
	2002–2003	Spring	218.61 (71)	202.71 (6)	15.9
	2003–2004	Fall	215.33 (84)	176.5 (10)	38.83
	2003–2004	Spring	220.54 (84)	190.8 (10)	29.74
	2004–2005	Fall	216.06 (63)	198.23 (13)	17.83
	2004–2005	Spring	219.58 (63)	200.31 (13)	19.27
	2005–2006	Fall	215.56 (55)	202.85 (13)	12.71
	2005–2006	Spring	220.84 (55)	208.75 (13)	12.09
7	2000–2001	Fall	220.01 (97)	204.73 (15)	15.28
	2000–2001	Spring	223.51 (97)	207.63 (15)	15.88
	2001–2002	Fall	221.36 (105)	205 (6)	16.36
	2001–2002	Spring	223.85 (105)	209.5 (6)	14.35
	2002–2003	Fall	220.52 (93)	199 (12)	21.52
	2002–2003	Spring	223.93 (93)	203.18 (12)	20.75
	2003–2004	Fall	216.82 (95)	197.7 (10)	19.12
	2003–2004	Spring	221.55 (95)	203.6 (10)	17.95
	2004–2005	Fall	221.04 (104)	186.5 (8)	34.54
	2004–2005	Spring	224.53 (104)	197.75 (8)	26.78
	2005–2006	Fall	221.55 (84)	199 (15)	22.55
	2005–2006	Spring	225.28 (84)	208.71 (15)	16.57

NWEA Reading MAP Gap Analysis *Continued*

Grade	Year	Term	MAP Score Non-EEN	MAP Score EEN	Gap
8	2000–2001 2000–2001	Fall Spring	227.94 (100) 228.38 (100)	204.44 (9) 209.91 (9)	23.5 18.47
	2001–2002 2001–2002	Fall Spring	224.83 (95) 227.53 (95)	200.76 (17) 199.25 (17)	24.07 28.28
	2002–2003 2002–2003	Fall Spring	225.85 (104) 230.02 (104)	208.67 (9) 210.5 (9)	17.18 19.52
	2003–2004 2003–2004	Fall Spring	225.26 (93) 227.5 (93)	206.2 (10) 212.22 (10)	19.06 15.28
	2004–2005 2004–2005	Fall Spring	223.53 (94) 228.22 (94)	207.31 (13) 211.17 (13)	16.22 17.05
	2005–2006 2005–2006	Fall Spring	226.82 (102) 230.24 (102)	202.44 (9) 209.3 (9)	24.38 20.94
9	2000–2001 2000–2001	Fall Spring	227.59 (96) 226.98 (96)	208.7 (10) 207.78 (10)	18.89 19.2
	2001–2002 2001–2002	Fall Spring	228.04 (96) 228.6 (96)	209.1 (10) 210.56 (10)	18.94 18.04
	2002–2003 2002–2003	Fall Spring	228.78 (93) 228.85 (93)	208.72 (18) 205.17 (18)	20.06 23.68
	2003–2004 2003–2004	Fall Spring	228.33 (117) 230.23 (117)	213 (8) 217 (8)	15.33 13.23
	2004–2005 2004–2005	Fall Spring	226.56 (96) 229.04 (96)	211.25 (8) 215.6 (8)	15.31 13.44
	2005–2006 2005–2006	Fall Spring	228.26 (92) 231.89 (92)	209.56 (9) 210.8 (9)	18.7 21.09
10	2000–2001 2000–2001	Fall Spring	231.65 (121) 231.65 (121)	204 (10) 207 (10)	27.65 24.65
	2001–2002 2001–2002	Fall Spring	228.2 (96) 230.52 (96)	209.33 (9) 210 (9)	18.87 20.52
	2002–2003 2002–2003	Fall Spring	232.85 (92) 233.58 (92)	212.28 (18) 214 (18)	20.57 19.58
	2003–2004 2003–2004	Fall Spring	229.68 (92) 229.98 (92)	205.17 (18) 210.63 (18)	24.51 19.35
	2004–2005 2004–2005	Fall Spring	229.36 (117) 233.01 (117)	221.11 (9) 217.5 (9)	8.25 15.51
	2005–2006 2005–2006	Fall Spring	231.1 (90) 234.2 (90)	213.5 (9) 216.7 (9)	17.6 17.5

Figures 8.4 and 8.5 report the WKCE state assessment language arts data over the last seven years and the mean language score on the MAP assessments. Figure 8.4 displays the percentage of students who performed at the proficient or advanced level and those who performed at the minimal or basic level. Figure 8.4 is coded to show matched cohort group performance and to easily identify whether the same group of students improved as they progressed through the grade levels. Figure 8.5 displays the mean RIT score in language by grade level and testing term, as well as the mean growth in language usage demonstrated each year by grade level.

From Figure 8.4, it is clear that the matched cohort from fourth (1999–2000) to eighth (2003–04) to tenth grade (2005–06) increased scores as they progressed through the grades. The matched cohort from fourth (2000–01) to eighth (2004–05) also improved. However, the matched cohort from fourth (2001–02) to eighth (2005–06) showed a decline in the percentage of students performing at the proficient or advanced level, from 81.40% to 80.61%. Also, in every instance of analyses from eighth to tenth grade in all years except 2000–01 to 2002–03 and 2003–04 to 2005–06, the matched cohort performance went down. Though the percentages of students performing at the proficient or advanced level are still outstanding, they are not what they should be, and this, too, will be analyzed in more detail at an upcoming Data Retreat.

The good news is that as the data is analyzed from year to year in one grade level, it is apparent that achievement is improving within grade levels. In the fourth grade, 83.58% of students performed at the proficient or advanced level during 1999–2000; that figure increased to 88.13% in 2005–06. The eighth grade displayed a downward trend, from 89.58% proficient or advanced during the 1999–2000 school year to 80.61% in 2005–06. The tenth grade, however, brought the language arts results back to the positive side, increasing from 82.88% proficient or advanced during the 1999–2000 school year to 85.13% in 2005–06.

Figure 8.4 Wisconsin Knowledge and Concepts Exam (WKCE) Language Results Grades 3 Through 8, and 10 for 1999–2000 Through 2005–2006

Grade	Performance Levels	1999–2000	2000–2001	2001–2002	2002–2003	2003–2004	2004–2005	2005–2006
3	Minimal and Basic							
	Proficient and Advanced	This Grade Not Tested with WKCE During These Years in This Subject						
	All							
4	Minimal and Basic	13.43%	19.40%	16.28%	14.29%	17.46%	10.96%	11.87%
	Proficient and Advanced	83.58%	79.10%	81.40%	84.29%	82.54%	89.04%	88.13%
	All	100.00%	100.00%	100.00%	100.00%	100.00%	100.00%	100.00%
5	Minimal and Basic							
	Proficient and Advanced							
	All							
6	Minimal and Basic	These Grades Not Tested with WKCE During These Years in This Subject						
	Proficient and Advanced							
	All							
7	Minimal and Basic							
	Proficient and Advanced							
	All							
8	Minimal and Basic	10.42%	18.69%	21.15%	13.39%	15.84%	17.14%	19.39%
	Proficient and Advanced	89.58%	81.31%	78.85%	86.61%	84.16%	82.86%	80.61%
	All	100.00%	100.00%	100.00%	100.00%	100.00%	100.00%	100.00%
10	Minimal and Basic	17.12%	22.14%	27.18%	14.41%	21.70%	14.05%	14.87%
	Proficient and Advanced	82.88%	77.86%	72.82%	85.59%	78.30%	85.95%	85.13%
	All	100.00%	100.00%	100.00%	100.00%	100.00%	100.00%	100.00%

Although the WKCE state test data do not show an increase in language arts performance at all grade levels, the MAP data suggest a different story. Though the percentages of proficient or advanced students may not have increased for the state test, there has been steady growth in language arts scores according to the MAP test. The mean growth scores for language usage over the last six years are highlighted in gray.

With the exception of grade 10, every grade level from the second through the ninth grade demonstrated an increase in growth from 2000–01 through 2005–06. One of the most outstanding examples is that the second grade went from 2.94 mean growth points in 2000–01 to 20.16 points mean growth during the 2005–06 school year. Unlike the results for the WKCE exam, the eighth grade showed growth gains over the last three years—from a mean growth of 2.76 points during the 2003–04 school year to 5.75 mean growth points during the 2005–06 school year. Another important piece of information to note here is that the mean scores went up from year to year for the fall and spring. In other words, students are coming in higher and leaving higher every year.

Figure 8.5. NWEA MAP Assessment
Language Growth Data by Grade Level

Grade	Term	2000–2001	2001–2002	2002–2003	2003–2004	2004–2005	2005–2006
2	Fall	184.36 (70)	182.63 (65)	178.32 (65)	180.75 (69)	179.18 (69)	179.14 (78)
	Spring	187.3 (70)	187.08 (65)	192.97 (65)	197.9 (69)	195.69 (69)	199.3 (78)
	Growth	2.94	4.45	14.65	17.15	16.51	20.16
3	Fall	199.41 (88)	192.73 (76)	191.75 (67)	194.21 (67)	198.26 (66)	191.91 (69)
	Spring	201.76 (88)	197.33 (76)	203.11 (67)	205.21 (67)	206.18 (66)	205.26 (69)
	Growth	2.35	4.6	11.36	11	7.92	13.35
4	Fall	207.94 (69)	202.45 (89)	202.4 (72)	201.64 (66)	203.89 (76)	203.78 (69)
	Spring	210.38 (69)	208.3 (89)	209.32 (72)	209.7 (66)	210.41 (76)	210.79 (69)
	Growth	2.44	5.85	6.92	8.06	6.52	7.01
5	Fall	211.18 (49)	210.27 (75)	210.38 (86)	207.57 (74)	207.71 (112)	209.97 (78)
	Spring	214.12 (49)	213.42 (75)	218.39 (86)	216.71 (74)	218.78 (112)	218.63 (78)
	Growth	2.94	3.15	8.01	9.14	11.07	8.66
6	Fall	218.89 (88)	216.51 (76)	212.5 (77)	216.3 (94)	214.68 (107)	217.04 (68)
	Spring	222.1 (88)	221.21 (76)	217.7 (77)	222.52 (94)	219.36 (107)	221.84 (68)
	Growth	3.21	4.7	5.2	6.22	4.68	4.8
7	Fall	222.6 (112)	224.12 (111)	220.58 (105)	218.36 (105)	221 (112)	220.69 (99)
	Spring	222.26 (112)	226.75 (111	223.83 (105)	223.5 (105)	225.01 (112)	224.06 (99)
	Growth	-0.34	2.63	3.25	5.14	4.01	3.37
8	Fall	226.21 (109)	222.94 (112)	227.48 (113)	225.58 (103)	223.01 (107)	224.9 (111)
	Spring	227.3 (109)	226.58 (112)	230.32 (113)	228.34 (103)	226.87 (107)	230.65 (111)
	Growth	1.09	3.64	2.84	2.76	3.86	5.75
9	Fall	228.11 (106)	226.72 (106)	225.09 (111)	227.88 (125)	226.4 (104	225.53 (101)
	Spring	229.07 (106)	227.49 (106)	227.23 (111)	228.99 (125)	226.63 (104)	227.43 (101)
	Growth	0.96	0.77	2.14	1.11	0.23	1.9
10	Fall	232.52 (131)	228.79 (105)	227.69 (110)	227.38 (110)	227.81 (126)	228.35 (99)
	Spring	234.05 (131)	230.22 (105)	231.18 (110)	227.01 (110)	228.11 (126)	228.45 (99)
	Growth	1.53	1.43	3.49	-0.37	0.3	0.1

Today, math instruction in our district looks dramatically different than it did in the fall of 1999. Multiple changes have been made at all levels (elementary school, middle school, and high school) in my district. In the middle school, beginning in 1999, the curriculum was dropped one full grade level. What had been seventh-grade math became sixth-grade math. What had been eighth-grade math became seventh-grade math. Adjustments were made to the fifth-grade math curriculum to prepare students to enter sixth-grade math, which actually tackled the seventh-grade math curriculum. Prealgebra and algebra were added to the seventh grade as course options. Algebra was expanded at the eighth-grade level from one section to three sections, and geometry was also added to the eighth-grade math curriculum. Dramatic changes were needed in our middle school curriculum because we were not challenging our highest-performing students.

After those curricular changes were made, we also needed to implement a remedial program in math because we still had a small group of students who were falling behind. The Math Matters program was created. Math Matters is a remedial math program designed exclusively around data. Students are selected for the program based on four criteria: classroom grades, MAP test scores, WKCE assessment scores, and teacher recommendations. If a student meets the criteria for selection, he or she is placed into the Math Matters program and receives supplemental math instruction based on his or her identified areas of need. Once a deficit area is addressed and the achievement gap in that area is closed, the student is dismissed from the program. (For more information on the Math Matters program, see Chapter 4, "Data Translation.")

Another change that was implemented in our district based on data was the development of areas of emphasis at each grade level and adjustments to the scope and sequencing of instruction. Each grade level has an area that it emphasizes every day of the school year, regardless of the lesson for the day. For example, first-grade teachers emphasize addition concepts in their classroom. Every day, they do addition problems to keep the skills fresh and at the forefront of their students' minds. The scope and sequencing of instruction were a little more difficult to change than implementing areas of emphasis. We encouraged teachers to teach the chapters in their math book out of order. At first, that idea was met with some resistance. But as time when on, the teachers realized that in order to focus their instruction on the data they had from assessments, they had to teach the chapters out of order. This happened in one of our fourth-grade classrooms. The teacher noticed that his students were doing quite well in the measurement strand of our state standards as measured by the MAP test. Measurement was the next chapter that he was to teach his students. He asked whether he could skip the measurement chapter and move on to the statistics and probability chapter because the scores of his students were not as high in that area. The response to that request was a resounding yes.

At the high school level, we found that we needed to add a remedial class for students who had slipped through the cracks while the changes were occurring at the elementary and middle school levels. Again based on data, we created a course that was implemented in the fall of 2005. Figures 8.6 and 8.7 depict the WKCE assessment math data over the last seven years and the mean math score on the MAP assessments. Figure 8.6 displays the percentage of students who performed at the proficient or advanced level and those who performed at the minimal or basic level. Figure 8.6 is coded to show matched cohort group performance and to easily identify whether the same group of students improved as they progressed through the grade levels. Figure 8.7 displays the mean RIT score in math by grade level and testing term, as well as the mean growth in math demonstrated each year by grade level.

The math results on the WKCE assessment show steady growth in the percentages of students performing at the proficient or advanced level for almost all matched cohort groups. An exception to the matched cohort growth is the fourth grade (1999–2000) to eighth grade (2003–04), which dropped from 83.33% proficient or advanced to 82.18%. However, that same matched cohort increased its performance to 89.11% proficient or advanced by their sophomore year (2005–06). The second matched cohort group that showed a slight decline in performance was the fourth grade (2002–03), with 85.71% proficient or advanced, to eighth grade (2005–06), with 84.13%. The biggest decline occurred between the 2004–05 fourth-grade students, who scored 91.78% proficient or advanced, to the 2005–06 fifth-grade students, who scored only 78.87% proficient or advanced. Obviously, the decline from fourth to fifth grade is the most concerning. Because the WKCE assessment had never been given in the fifth grade before the 2005–06 school year, the belief is that we may need to address some curricular issues in the fourth grade. Wisconsin administers its state test at the end of October, so more analysis is needed of the fourth-grade curriculum from October until the end of the year and the fifth-grade curriculum in September and October.

Overall, however, most of the matched cohort groups progressed nicely. The state benchmark in math for the 2005–06 school year was 47.5% proficient or advanced. In all grade levels, we are well above that benchmark. The performance of the same grade levels over time shows a steady increase in the percentages of students performing at the proficient or advanced level, with very few exceptions. Even though we have a few bumps in the road here and there, overall, the percentage of proficient or advanced students on the math portion of the WKCE exam is showing improvement.

Figure 8.6. Wisconsin Knowledge and Concepts Exam (WKCE) Math Results for Grades 3 Through 8 and 10 for 1999–2000 Through 2005–2006

Grade	Performance Level	1999–2000	2000–2001	2001–2002	2002–2003	2003–2004	2004–2005	2005–2006
3	Minimal and Basic							9.98%
	Proficient and Advanced	This Grade Not Tested with WKCE During These Years						90.02%
	All							100.00%
4	Minimal and Basic	13.64%	31.34%	23.26%	12.86%	19.05%	8.22%	16.34%
	Proficient and Advanced	83.33%	67.16%	74.42%	85.71%	80.95%	91.78%	83.66%
	All	100.00%	100.00%	100.00%	100.00%	100.00%	100.00%	100.00%
5	Minimal and Basic							23.13%
	Proficient and Advanced							76.87%
	All							100.00%
6	Minimal and Basic	These Grades Not Tested with WKCE During These Years						13.38%
	Proficient and Advanced							86.62%
	All							100.00%
7	Minimal and Basic							15.87%
	Proficient and Advanced							84.13%
	All							100.00%
8	Minimal and Basic	39.58%	31.78%	33.65%	10.71%	17.82%	12.38%	10.89%
	Proficient and Advanced	60.42%	64.49%	62.50%	89.29%	82.18%	87.62%	89.11%
	All	100.00%	100.00%	100.00%	100.00%	100.00%	100.00%	100.00%
10	Minimal and Basic	47.75%	22.90%	26.21%	18.92%	23.58%	12.40%	10.89%
	Proficient and Advanced	52.25%	77.10%	73.79%	81.08%	76.42%	87.60%	89.11%
	All	100.00%	100.00%	100.00%	100.00%	100.00%	100.00%	100.00%

As was the case when comparing the WKCE language arts results to the MAP language results earlier in this chapter, the MAP data for math shown reported in Figure 8.7 seem to provide a clearer picture of math performance by grade level. All tested grade levels demonstrated higher growth during the 2005–06 school year than they had during the 2000–01 school year. It is also worth noting that six of the nine grade levels produced higher spring scores in 2005–06 than in 2000–01. Additionally, every grade level has performed above the expected grade-level mean since 2002–03, with the seventh, eighth, ninth, and tenth grades exceeding their expected grade-level means from 2000–01 onward.

The changes that we have made to our math curriculum and programming options based on the use and analysis of data have paid dividends in the math performance of our students. We are convinced that this is directly attributable to our use of data to drive instructional decisions and program development. Teachers used their assessment data and classroom data to adjust what was happening in their classrooms, and it is clear that the true beneficiaries of that practice have been our students.

Figure 8.7. NWEA MAP Assessment
Math Growth Data by Grade Level

Grade	Term	2000–2001	2001–2002	2002–2003	2003–2004	2004–2005	2005–2006
2	Fall	185.01 (70)	180.09 (65)	179.06 (65)	178.12 (69)	181.12 (69)	180.99 (78)
	Spring	187.78 (70)	187.38 (65)	191.44 (65)	199.5 (69)	196.54 (69)	199.89 (78)
	Growth	2.77	7.29	12.38	21.38	15.42	18.9
3	Fall	194.84 (88)	191.18 (76)	192.15 (67)	194.05 (67)	197.2 (66)	193 (69)
	Spring	199.02 (88)	198.42 (76)	204.14 (67)	206.35 (67)	207.82 (66)	206.68 (69)
	Growth	4.18	7.24	11.99	12.3	10.62	13.68
4	Fall	204.94 (69)	199.29 (89)	201.64 (72)	203.34 (66)	204.92 (76)	205.23 (69)
	Spring	208.04 (69)	208.65 (89)	209.27 (72)	213.41 (66)	214.74 (76)	211.85 (69)
	Growth	3.1	9.36	7.63	10.07	9.82	6.62
5	Fall	211.45 (49)	209.45 (75)	207.76 (86)	209.37 (74)	211.98 (67)	212.12 (78)
	Spring	215.55 (49)	216.15 (75)	219.77 (86)	218.04 (74)	220.32 (67)	222.76 (78)
	Growth	4.1	6.7	12.01	8.67	8.34	10.64
6	Fall	218.54 (88)	217.58 (76)	216.43 (77)	216.27 (94)	217.29 (76)	220.25 (68)
	Spring	223.88 (88)	223.69 (76)	224.41 (77)	225.93 (94)	225.64 (76)	230.09 (68)
	Growth	5.34	6.11	7.98	9.66	8.35	9.84
7	Fall	229.94 (112)	227.19 (111)	224.57 (105)	222.09 (105)	227.46 (112)	226.86 (99)
	Spring	234.32 (112)	236.56 (111)	234.17 (105)	229.99 (105)	234.88 (112)	233.39 (99)
	Growth	4.38	9.37	9.6	7.9	7.42	6.53
8	Fall	236.17 (109)	233.24 (112)	237.44 (113)	235.14 (103)	231.41 (107)	235.32 (111)
	Spring	239.36 (109)	237.83 (112)	243.21 (113)	239.49 (103)	237.28 (107)	239.35 (111)
	Growth	3.19	4.59	5.77	4.35	5.87	4.03
9	Fall	242.92 (106)	241.2 (106)	238.22 (111)	240.42 (125)	237.86 (104)	239.57 (101)
	Spring	243.14 (106)	243.45 (106)	241.06 (111)	244.05 (125)	241.07 (104)	244.42 (101)
	Growth	0.22	2.25	2.84	3.63	3.21	4.85
10	Fall	247.01 (131)	245.52 (105)	244.64 (110)	242.04 (110)	242.59	241.06 (99)
	Spring	247.85 (131)	249.58 (105)	246.97 (110)	245.62 (110)	246.08	243.99 (99)
	Growth	0.84	4.06	2.33	3.58	3.49	2.93

In the fall of 2004–05, when we began to service special education students identified with either a learning disability or an emotional or behavioral disability through our Title I reading program, we also began to service those students through our remedial math program—Math Matters—if they also had an identified math need. This concept was also an outcome of our Data Retreat during the summer of 2004. The special education teachers who also served on the District Leadership Team believed that other staff members were better qualified to teach their students mathematics. From that summer onward, we have included special education students in our remedial programs in both reading and math. The data in Figure 8.8 reveal that the restructuring of our math programs has had a dramatic effect on students' performance in the area of math as well.

As Figure 8.8 makes clear, the gap between students in special education programs and those in regular education programs has decreased impressively over the last six years. The second-grade gap in reading achievement decreased from 15 points in the fall of 2000 to 1.6 points in the spring of 2006, making the achievement gap between regular education students and special education students at that grade level almost nonexistent. That is an incredible decrease that we fully attribute to our use of data to drive instructional practices in the classroom and our expansion of programs to provide assistance to students who would otherwise not receive such services. In the third grade, the math gap decreased from 13.6 points in the fall of 2000 to 5.78 points in the spring of 2006, but in the fourth grade, it increased from 3.98 points in the fall of 2000 to 7.62 points in the spring of 2006. This increase would seem to substantiate the WKCE math data, which showed a decline between the fourth-grade and fifth-grade WKCE assessments in math. This suggests to me that something is occurring in fourth-grade math classes or in the fourth-grade math curriculum that needs to be analyzed in more depth—and will be at an upcoming Data Retreat. The fifth-grade data show that the math gap dropped from 18.2 points in the fall of 2000 to 14.1 points in the spring of 2006, and in the sixth grade, it fell from 19.4 points in the fall of 2000 to 12.4 points in the spring of 2006. The seventh-grade data, like the fifth-grade data, show an increase in the achievement gap between students with disabilities and nondisabled students from the fall of 2000 to the spring of 2006, another finding that will be addressed during an upcoming Data Retreat. Overall, however, the math achievement gap between nondisabled students and students with disabilities in my district has closed at almost all grade levels.

Figure 8.8. NWEA Math MAP Gap Analysis

Grade	Year	Term	MAP Score Non-EEN	MAP Score EEN	Gap
2	2000–2001	Fall	187.38 (62)	172.42 (8)	15
	2000–2001	Spring	190.45 (62)	173.5 (8)	17
	2001–2002	Fall	180.24 (50)	179.6 (15)	0.64
	2001–2002	Spring	189.88 (50)	178.07 (15)	11.8
	2002–2003	Fall	179.5 (57)	174.83 (8)	4.67
	2002–2003	Spring	192.49 (57)	184.25 (8)	8.24
	2003–2004	Fall	178.48 (62)	174.33 (7)	4.15
	2003–2004	Spring	199.49 (62)	199.57 (7)	-0.1
	2004–2005	Fall	181.54 (62)	177.43 (7)	4.11
	2004–2005	Spring	197.6 (62)	188.13 (7)	9.47
	2005–2006	Fall	181.2 (64)	179.92 (14)	1.28
	2005–2006	Spring	200.14 (64)	198.54 (14)	1.6
3	2000–2001	Fall	196.23 (79)	182.67 (9)	13.6
	2000–2001	Spring	200.33 (79)	186 (9)	14.3
	2001–2002	Fall	192.48 (62)	185.43 (14)	7.05
	2001–2002	Spring	199.66 (62)	193.21 (14)	6.45
	2002–2003	Fall	192.98 (54)	188.93 (13)	4.05
	2002–2003	Spring	204.62 (54)	201.82 (13)	2.8
	2003–2004	Fall	195.35 (58)	185.78 (9)	9.57
	2003–2004	Spring	207.54 (58)	198.56 (9)	8.98
	2004–2005	Fall	198.78 (55)	189.45 (11)	9.33
	2004–2005	Spring	208.96 (55)	202.18 (11)	6.78
	2005–2006	Fall	194.34 (58)	185.91 (11)	8.43
	2005–2006	Spring	207.6 (58)	201.82 (11)	5.78
4	2000–2001	Fall	205.8 (61)	198.38 (8)	3.98
	2000–2001	Spring	208.89 (61)	201.5 (8)	7.39
	2001–2002	Fall	200.96 (77)	188.58 (12)	12.4
	2001–2002	Spring	209.92 (77)	199.3 (12)	10.6
	2002–2003	Fall	202.95 (63)	193.4 (9)	9.55
	2002–2003	Spring	210.42 (63)	201.8 (9)	8.62
	2003–2004	Fall	204.42 (56)	197.4 (10)	7.02
	2003–2004	Spring	214.13 (56)	209.11 (10)	5.02
	2004–2005	Fall	206.06 (67)	196.44 (9)	9.62
	2004–2005	Spring	215.78 (67)	205.88 (9)	9.9
	2005–2006	Fall	206.61 (59)	199.31 (10)	7.3
	2005–2006	Spring	213.2 (59)	205.58 (10)	7.62

Grade	Year	Term	MAP Score Non-EEN	MAP Score EEN	Gap
5	2000–2001 2000–2001	Fall Spring	214.4 (37) 219.19 (37)	196.23 (12) 196.77 (12)	18.2 22.4
	2001–2002 2001–2002	Fall Spring	211.58 (65) 218.09 (65)	195.6 (10) 203.7 (10)	16 14.4
	2002–2003 2002–2003	Fall Spring	211.34 (76) 222.65 (76)	182.73 (10) 199.64 (10)	28.6 23
	2003–2004 2003–2004	Fall Spring	210.41 (65) 219.43 (65)	202.5 (9) 208.7 (9)	7.91 10.7
	2004–2005 2004–2005	Fall Spring	212.65 (56) 222.83 (56)	205.6 (11) 209.25 (11)	7.05 13.6
	2005–2006 2005–2006	Fall Spring	213.9 (67) 224.35 (67)	198.44 (10) 210.22 (10)	15.5 14.1
6	2000–2001 2000–2001	Fall Spring	220.5 (79) 225.8 (79)	201.11 (9) 206.56 (9)	19.4 19.2
	2001–2002 2001–2002	Fall Spring	219.42 (66) 225.94 (66)	205.4 (10) 207.9 (10)	14 18
	2002–2003 2002–2003	Fall Spring	218.11 (71) 226.35 (71)	196.83 (6) 201.17 (6)	21.3 25.2
	2003–2004 2003–2004	Fall Spring	219.18 (84) 228.62 (84)	192.1 (10) 203.9 (10)	27.1 24.7
	2004–2005 2004–2005	Fall Spring	219.19 (63) 228.75 (63)	208.08 (13) 213 (13)	11.1 15.8
	2005–2006 2005–2006	Fall Spring	222.73 (55) 232.13 (55)	209.77 (13) 219.73 (13)	13 12.4
7	2000–2001 2000–2001	Fall Spring	232.14 (97) 236.28 (97)	213.77 (15) 218.17 (15)	18.4 18.1
	2001–2002 2001–2002	Fall Spring	228.88 (105) 237.76 (105)	201.86 (6) 213.67 (6)	27 24.1
	2002–2003 2002–2003	Fall Spring	226.51 (93) 236.41 (93)	209.25 (12) 217.25 (12)	17.3 19.2
	2003–2004 2003–2004	Fall Spring	224.84 (95) 232.79 (95)	195.9 (10) 203.4 (10)	28.9 29.4
	2004–2005 2004–2005	Fall Spring	228.74 (104) 236.33 (104)	210.75 (8) 217.25 (8)	18 19.1
	2005–2006 2005–2006	Fall Spring	229.78 (84) 236.57 (84)	207.54 (15) 213.86 (15)	22.2 22.7

Figure 8.8. NWEA Math MAP Gap Analysis *Continued*

Grade	Year	Term	MAP Score Non-EEN	MAP Score EEN	Gap
8	2000–2001 2000–2001	Fall Spring	238.73 (100) 241.95 (100)	214.83 (9) 215.55 (9)	23.9 26.4
	2001–2002 2001–2002	Fall Spring	237.38 (95) 242.36 (95)	210.12 (17) 211.19 (17)	27.3 31.2
	2002–2003 2002–2003	Fall Spring	239.28 (104) 245.57 (104)	216 (9) 218.4 (9)	23.3 27.2
	2003–2004 2003–2004	Fall Spring	237.14 (93) 241.2 (93)	216.7 (10) 222 (10)	20.4 19.2
	2004–2005 2004–2005	Fall Spring	234.85 (94) 240.53 (94)	206.54 (13) 212.33 (13)	28.3 28.2
	2005–2006 2005–2006	Fall Spring	236.87 (102) 241.06 (102)	217.67 (9) 221.7 (9)	19.2 19.4
9	2000–2001 2000–2001	Fall Spring	245.57 (96) 245.53 (96)	217.5 (10) 220.2 (10)	28.1 25.3
	2001–2002 2001–2002	Fall Spring	243.13 (96) 245.79 (96)	222.9 (10) 218.78 (10)	20.2 27
	2002–2003 2002–2003	Fall Spring	242.49 (93) 245.08 (93)	216.39 (18) 220.33 (18)	26.1 24.8
	2003–2004 2003–2004	Fall Spring	241.86 (117) 245.45 (117)	219.38 (8) 224.5 (8)	22.5 21
	2004–2005 2004–2005	Fall Spring	239.73 (96) 243.13 (96)	215.38 (8) 221.1 (8)	24.4 22
	2005–2006 2005–2006	Fall Spring	242.4 (92) 246.94 (92)	210.67 () 221 (9)	31.7 25.9
10	2000–2001 2000–2001	Fall Spring	249.2 (121) 250.58 (121)	220.7 (10) 215.6 (10)	28.5 35
	2001–2002 2001–2002	Fall Spring	247.71 (96) 251.78 (96)	221.89 (9) 226.67 (9)	25.8 25.1
	2002–2003 2002–2003	Fall Spring	249.63 (92) 252.11 (92)	219.44 (18) 222.11 (18)	30.2 30
	2003–2004 2003–2004	Fall Spring	246.76 (92) 250.11 (92)	217.89 (18) 223.89 (18)	28.9 26.2
	2004–2005 2004–2005	Fall Spring	243.63 (117) 248.16 (117)	229.22 (9) 226.67 (9)	14.4 21.5
	2005–2006 2005–2006	Fall Spring	243.13 (90) 246.48 (90)	222.6 (9) 222.6 (9)	20.5 23.9

For the past several years, the focus in our district has been on reading and math and the integration of those subject areas into other content areas. For example, our art department worked on math skills and integrated geometry and measurement concepts into its art instruction. The music department also worked on math concepts using whole notes, half notes, and quarter notes in sheet music to work on fractions. Our physical education department has taken advantage of the DDIS model for school improvement by adding more reading assignments to its curriculum, using reading strategies to help students get the most out of articles on current events in health and kinesiology. Our science department firmly believed that if they spent time working on reading using the science curriculum, science assessment scores would improve. In fact, the science department in my district has compiled a list of vocabulary words that are specific to that content area and has created its own pre-test and post-test assessments to measure mastery of understanding—not only for science-specific vocabulary but also for science concepts as well.

Figure 8.9 displays the WKCE assessment data for my district in the area of science. Historically, our district has scored extremely well in science achievement. In almost every year, the percentage of students achieving at the proficient or advanced level on the WKCE exam has hovered between 80% and 96% at all grade levels. There are a few exceptions to this outstanding performance in the eighth and tenth grades, when adjustments were made to curriculum. We do not yet have enough MAP data related to science to include that data in our performance measures.

An unexpected benefit of using data to drive instruction in the classroom has been the willingness of staff members, particularly in our science department, to use their collaboration time for professional learning and their own learning. They have been reading school improvement literature, seeking out resources related on teaching practices in science related to areas in need of improvement, and even obtaining additional course content in order to design their own lab books and assessments. The science department is one group of district leaders that has embraced the DDIS model, moving through all of the components of the model and not only analyzing assessment data but actually designing their own standardized assessment to test their students in areas of need identified in the data.

Figure 8.9. Wisconsin Knowledge and Concepts Exam (WKCE) Science Results

Grade	Performance Levels	1999–2000	2000–2001	2001–2002	2002–2003	2003–2004	2004–2005	2005–2006
3	Minimal and Basic							
	Proficient and Advanced	This Grade Not Tested with WKCE During These Years						
	All							
4	Minimal and Basic	4.48%	17.91%	8.14%	8.57%	11.11%	9.59%	3.87%
	Proficient and Advanced	95.52%	82.09%	91.86%	91.43%	88.89%	90.41%	96.13%
	All	100.00%	100.00%	100.00%	100.00%	100.00%	100.00%	100.00%
5	Minimal and Basic							
	Proficient and Advanced							
	All							
6	Minimal and Basic	These Grades Not Tested with WKCE During These Years						
	Proficient and Advanced							
	All							
7	Minimal and Basic							
	Proficient and Advanced							
	All							
8	Minimal and Basic	17.71%	24.30%	27.88%	7.14%	8.91%	11.43%	7.68%
	Proficient and Advanced	82.29%	75.70%	72.12%	92.86%	91.09%	88.57%	92.32%
	All	100.00%	100.00%	100.00%	100.00%	100.00%	100.00%	100.00%
10	Minimal and Basic	33.33%	18.32%	24.27%	15.32%	20.75%	8.26%	10.89%
	Proficient and Advanced	66.67%	81.68%	75.73%	84.68%	79.25%	91.74%	89.11%
	All	100.00%	100.00%	100.00%	100.00%	100.00%	100.00%	100.00%

Figure 8.10 illustrates our students' performance on the social studies section of our WKCE assessment. As in science, our social studies scores have been outstanding for several consecutive years. The percentage of students performing at the proficient or advanced level has consistently been above 80% at all grade levels, typically in the range of 85% to 95%. Even at this performance level, our social studies department is still focusing its efforts on improving instruction. Typically, there is a great deal of reading involved in the content area of social studies. Our social studies teachers determined that they needed to find a better way to teach all of the students in their classrooms and differentiate their instruction. Some of the social studies department members were trained in the use of the Sheltered Instructional Observation Protocol (SIOP). After the training, the teachers came back to the district and trained their fellow department members on how to use SIOP to differentiate instruction in the classroom. Each month, the teachers tried another strategy in their classes and reported back to department members on the success of their lessons. A consistent focus on improving instruction in order to meet the identified needs of all students is what drives our district. Using data to drive instruction in my district is an expectation, not an exception.

Figure 8.10 Wisconsin Knowledge and Concepts Exam Social Studies Results, Grades 3–8 and Grade 10, 1999–2000 to 2005–06

Grade	Performance Levels	1999–2000	2000–2001	2001–2002	2002–2003	2003–2004	2004–2005	2005–2006
3	Minimal and Basic							
	Proficient and Advanced	This Grade Not Tested with WKCE During These Years in This Subject						
	All							
4	Minimal and Basic	4.48%	17.91%	10.47%	1.43%	1.59%	1.37%	2.73%
	Proficient and Advanced	95.52%	82.09%	89.53%	98.57%	98.41%	98.63%	97.27%
	All	100.00%	100.00%	100.00%	100.00%	100.00%	100.00%	100.00%
5	Minimal and Basic							
	Proficient and Advanced							
	All							
6	Minimal and Basic	These Grades Not Tested with WKCE During These Years in This Subject						
	Proficient and Advanced							
	All							
7	Minimal and Basic							
	Proficient and Advanced							
	All							
8	Minimal and Basic	2.08%	9.35%	9.62%	1.79%	2.97%	10.48%	5.13%
	Proficient and Advanced	97.92%	90.65%	89.42%	98.21%	97.03%	89.52%	94.87%
	All	100.00%	100.00%	100.00%	100.00%	100.00%	100.00%	100.00%
10	Minimal and Basic	8.11%	6.11%	14.56%	9.91%	9.43%	11.57%	9.35%
	Proficient and Advanced	91.89%	93.89%	85.44%	90.09%	90.57%	88.43%	90.65%
	All							

The continued success of our district over the past seven years as depicted in this chapter demonstrates that using the DDIS model for school improvement does improve student achievement. The DDIS model provides districts with a framework that can guide their school improvement efforts. The components of the DDIS model—data collection, data reflection, data translation, data-driven instructional design, design feedback, and summative and formative assessment—help us organize all of the improvement efforts in our district.

Data collection in our district is constantly changing. As we analyze some of the data we have and design and implement more programs based on data, there are more data to collect. Systems and protocols for the collection of data must constantly change as well, so that any new data becomes incorporated into the process of collection. Data collection is the most critical component of the DDIS model. If inaccurate data are collected, recorded, stored, and analyzed, dire mistakes can be made. For example, a simple yet real data-collection error occurred in a nearby district when the genders of their students were missing or incorrectly entered into the Student Information System. When the district started to analyze its data, it discovered that it had 750 students with unknown gender. Imagine analyzing state-level assessment data and identifying an achievement gap between males and females. Because the data suggested there was an achievement gap related to gender, the district designed specific focus groups of male and female students to begin discussing this issue. Plans were being developed to offer gender-specific courses, only to discover that the data on which all of these actions had been based were incorrect. Knowing this statistic was incorrect, the district investigated the problem and found out that in many cases, the person who entered the data at the school level did not enter gender as part of the information. Once that problem was discovered, it was corrected and a data-entry process was developed.

Data collection sounds simple, but it is the component of the DDIS model that requires the most time up front when implementing a data-driven school improvement initiative. In fact, the collection and cleansing of data should begin about a year before the district actually moves forward with the data-driven initiative. Data collection is the backbone of any data-driven initiative, and it can make or break school improvement efforts. Any decisions based on data that are incomplete or inaccurate can negatively affect the school district, the students, and the credibility of the data-driven initiative.

It is important for school districts that are considering implementing a data-driven initiative to gather people from around the district and discuss which data should be collected before implementing any change. The first time districts go through this "data discovery" process, they cannot expect to think of everything they may possibly want to collect. That is why additional data types may need to be added to the data-collection process or protocol as districts work through the implementation of the DDIS model. For example, when we began to identify the data that we wanted to collect, we did not have our Math Matters program in place. When we added that remedial math program, we needed to adjust the data that we were collecting.

Districts also need to discuss how the data will be collected and who will be responsible for the collection. At this stage of the data-driven implementation, do not assume that people will automatically think to add data from a new program into the data-collection process. Someone—a data champion in the district—must relentlessly follow through on every single step of the process if the district is to move forward using the DDIS model.

The second component of the DDIS model, data reflection, is also critical for districts that want to implement a data-driven school improvement initiative. Teachers need to be given time to reflect on the data they have on their students. There are several ways to do this, such as providing time for professional learning days, early release days, and Data Retreats; bringing in substitute teachers while teachers do concentrated data analysis work; and providing daily stipends for work during the summer. Any creative way that a district can provide teachers with additional time is helpful. Districts implementing a DDIS model for school improvement need to avoid making the analysis of data "one more thing" that teachers need to complete on their own time. If the district believes the data-driven initiative is valuable for school improvement, it must be willing to back up that commitment by providing teachers with time and making the analysis of data a priority.

The data translation component of the DDIS model is the point at which the data are translated into program and curriculum changes. Data translation typically starts at the district level, as curriculum specialists identify gaps, overlaps, and performance deficits for specific subgroup of students. Once the problems are identified, it is time to get the teaching staff involved in the development of a solution. Do program changes need to be made? Do new programs need to be created? Should existing programs be changed or discontinued? An example of translating data into change that occurred in our district was our addition of a school breakfast program. For two years, during the summer Data Retreat, the District Leadership Team believed there was a correlation between students' performance on the MAP tests and whether they were hungry when they took the tests. We implemented a breakfast program during the 2005–06 school year and saw an increase of 2–10 points from fall to spring (depending on the grade level) in math scores on the MAP tests for students who received free or reduced meals, including breakfast. The students take the MAP assessments as early in the morning as we can schedule them, but approximately 50% of the children were testing on empty stomachs. It is too early to tell what the long-term effects of our breakfast program will be, but it seems to be off to a tremendous start.

Other outcomes of data translation in our district include the creation and implementation of our Math Matters program, the expansion of our Title I reading services to the middle school, the addition of guided reading in kindergarten through the second grade, the addition of algebra at the seventh-grade level, the addition of geometry at the eighth-grade level, major adjustments to the middle school math curriculum, the creation and implementation of a new Math 9 remedial math program at the high school, and the implementation of Word of the Week (WOW) and reading strategies in the content area meetings at the middle school. As the data suggest improvements, we create and implement them. The DDIS model, though it may appear stationary in the graphic depiction, is in constant motion. In a district that is successfully implementing the DDIS model, data are collected daily through multiple sources, reflected on at several levels, and transformed into change all the time.

Data-driven instructional design, the fourth component of the DDIS model, moves the use of data from the program-evaluation level (data translation) to the classroom level. In this component, classroom teachers plan and design lessons based on the data that are available to them. Providing teachers with access to data is essential when working through this component. Teachers need to have direct access to their data or know exactly where to go or who to ask to get the data they need for planning. Again, providing classroom teachers with time to do this so that they can design tiered lessons or differentiate their instruction based on the performance of the students in their classroom is vital. A template for a tiered lesson plan (Appendix B) and samples of completed tiered lesson plans (Appendices C, D, and E) are included at the end of this book. Encouraging and supporting teachers in their efforts to use data to inform and adjust their classroom instruction in order to meet the needs of all students is the ultimate goal of a data-driven school improvement initiative.

The design feedback component of the DDIS model allows district officials to adjust current and ongoing initiatives based on results and evaluate how information is being shared with the many stakeholders in a school district: students, parents, teachers, administrators, school board members, and the community. Not only educating teachers in the analysis and interpretation of data but also informing other stakeholders in the district about student achievement is key to the success of a data-driven initiative. Students in particular need to see how they have grown over time. They need to be data natives and understand that they are expected to meet their individually designed growth targets. A wonderful example of this occurred in my district as I was walking through the halls of our elementary school building. A third-grade student saw me and called out, "Hey, Dr. Blink, I just got a 222 on my language test and my target score was a 217!" When students understand that they have met and exceeded their growth targets for the year, one can almost be assured that this child's parents will understand as well.

Community members, school board members, and other interested stakeholders in the district need to be kept informed about the progress of the data-driven initiative and how it is affecting student achievement. There are several ways to accomplish this. Informational articles in local newspapers, academic retreats with school board members, informational meetings for parents, school district newsletters, and success stories on the district Web site are a few of the ways that school districts can make the design feedback component of the DDIS model an integral part of the process.

Summative and formative assessment is the final component of the DDIS model. It is the last piece because all districts have summative data. Summative data, by definition, provide a way to access information after a period of time. All of the state assessments administered as part of the NCLB requirements are summative assessments. Every district has those data—at a minimum. However, not all districts use formative assessments. In order for a school district to truly follow the DDIS model of school improvement, it must have at least one form of formative assessment in place. Teachers and administrators have to wrap their arms around the concept that assessment should be used at the beginning of instructional units, as well as at the end. When a formative assessment is given at the beginning of a unit or lesson of instruction, the data provided by that assessment give the classroom teacher valuable information about how to adjust his or her instruction to meet the needs of the children in a particular class.

9
Conclusion

How to Get Started

Where should a district begin? First, a conversation about whether the district is willing to make the commitment to a data-driven initiative must take place. Districts that are willing to undertake a data-driven initiative must be willing to question and reflect on their own thoughts and actions. They must be willing to create leaders at the teacher level, and they must not be afraid to listen to what those teacher-leaders have to say. When working with a Data-Driven Instructional System (DDIS) model for school improvement, everyone's opinion, hypothesis, or theory is worthwhile. A culture of mutual respect must exist among all members of the District Leadership Team, regardless of role or district responsibility.

Using the DDIS model for school improvement in a district will improve student achievement. Though it is not an easy undertaking, investing the time and effort to structure a school district using the DDIS model as a guide will pay dividends in the one area that educators are constantly focused on—the teaching and learning of children. Using data to drive instructional decisions and implementing the DDIS model is not just doing things right...it is the right thing to do for children. Imagine a world in which students are taught at a level at which they can understand and grow and those successes are celebrated. Every child can learn if the correct system is in place to guide and inform their instruction.

Let's think back to Paul, whom you met in the introduction to this book. If Paul were attending a school in a district that followed the DDIS model, he would receive classroom instruction that meets his needs. He would not be spending his time mopping floors, wiping off tables in the commons, or filling soda machines. Paul's teachers would be analyzing and interpreting the data that they have on Paul and planning his instruction accordingly. Paul's teachers would collaborate to design a plan of instruction that would meet his needs. Paul's self-confidence and self-esteem would increase because he would actually be learning something instead of completing nonacademic tasks. Imagine the self-satisfaction that Paul would feel on his 16th birthday if he could actually read the birthday cards he received without help from his parents! It is our job as educators to teach children—all children. We need to take that commitment seriously and teach all students instead of giving up on them. If we, as educators, do not believe that every child can learn something, then who will?

As I said in the introduction to this book, Paul's programming looks dramatically different now than it did before the No Child Left Behind requirements were put into place. Paul is in regular classes now, and he is actually learning to read. He still spends some time in his special education classroom, but instead of wiping tables and filling soda machines, Paul is working on his homework with assistance. I am a witness to the changes in Paul's self-esteem. He is playing on the high school football team now, he has more friends, and he does not suffer the teasing that he did when he could not read a word. Instead, other students help him with words when he struggles. He related an experience to me that I would like to share with you. At the end of the 2005–06 school year, Paul saw a word on a sign in the commons that he did not know. He asked one of his friends to help him understand the word and its meaning. His friend helped him read and understand the word without teasing him about it. Paul felt pretty good about that. The word was *commencement*. Now Paul knows that commencement and graduation mean just about the same thing, and he can read the word when he sees it. He still cannot compete with his grade-level peers academically, but he is making progress—progress that would never have occurred without the external pressure of No Child Left Behind.

Following the DDIS model for school improvement requires organization and commitment on the part of the district. Follow the examples set forth in this book as a guide. They will provide your school improvement initiative with reference points as you move through the process. There are four keys to a successful data-driven initiative: purpose, focus, communication and coordination, and follow-through. Be clear about the purpose and reasons for doing something. There are no secrets in school improvement initiatives. Limit the focus to one or two things. Do not try to do too much at one time. Communication and coordination is essential. Make sure everyone knows what is going on, why it is being done, and when it should be done. Relentless efforts to follow through must occur. If teachers are asked to do something, they must understand why they are doing it, how it relates to the entire initiative, and what is the merit of the task. If they are asked to do something that is never discussed, they will fail to see the value in completing the task at all.

The more information that is available on a child, the more that information should be used to make intelligent decisions about that child. When you really think about it…No Child Left Behind should not be seen as a threatening external pressure placed on schools—it should be seen as an opportunity to improve our schools and districts so that we can provide all children the education they deserve. Information is power! The more teachers know about the children in their classrooms, the more powerful they will feel to make a difference in the life of every child.

Appendix A

SASIxp
Data-Entry Protocol

The following is a list of fields that should be entered when setting up a new student.

Page 1

- Last name (if the name has a space—i.e., Van Oss—put the space in)
- First name
- Full middle name (no initials)
- Grade
- Gender
- Student ID (allow SASIxp to assign this identification number randomly—do not change)
- Mailing address (no abbreviations)
- City
- State
- Zip code
- Parent/guardian name
- Telephone number
- Birth date
- Social Security number
- Ethnicity
- Enter date
- Enter code
- OrgEntDate
- Code
- EntGrd
- Yr/Grad
- Advisor number (homeroom teacher all buildings)
- Advisor name (homeroom/care break teacher)
- ESL level

Page 2

- Birthplace: City and state or country of birth—e.g., Cancun, Mexico, or Chilton, Wisconsin. No abbreviations—spell out all words
- Locker
- Dist/Res: District of residence
- Sch/Res: School of residence
- Apport%: Enter 1 if the student is a full-time student; see drop-down list for other percentages
- Lst/Sch
- Ctz: U.S. Citizen (yes or no)—"Yes" for most
- Prim/Lang: Primary language—English for most
- Home/Lang: Language spoken at home—English for most
- CorrLang: Same as Prim/Lang and Home/Lang fields

Page 3

- User Code 6 (Open Enrolled Out): "Not" for most students, but you will need to change "Open Enrolled Out" students after you get information from district office
- User Code 7 (Open Enrolled In): "Not" for most students, but you will need to change "Open Enrolled In" students after you get information from district office
- User Code 8 (In District Full Year): "Yes" for most students (Yes = in district since third Friday count of previous school year)
- User Code 9 (In School Full Year): "Yes" for most students (change only if the student is not in school for the full year)

Reminder: "Open Enrolled Out" students need to be registered and then inactivated!

Appendix B

Example of a Tiered Lesson Plan for 8th-Grade Mathematics

Teacher:	Mr. Data Driven
Grade Level:	8
Academic Area:	Mathematics

Lesson Title/Summary:
Creedence Clearwater Revival is performing a concert in the Wildwood Middle School gym. All proceeds from the concert will benefit Dignity House for their new addition. Dignity House helps abused women and children.
Prior to the event, much planning must take place and everyone needs to do their part. Each of you will be given a task to complete to assist in the planning.

Standards Addressed:
A.8.1, A.8.2, A.8.4, A.8.5, D.8.1, D.8.3, D.8.4, E.8.1, E.8.2, E.8.4, F.8.1, F.8.2

Lowest Performing Students	Middle Performing Students	Highest Performing Students
Reme Dial Istilla Matter Beggin Forhelp	Rest of Class (Groupings of 3)	I.M. Bright Anita Challenge Justin Rich
NWEA Objective Strand	NWEA Objective Strand	NWEA Objective Strand
Mathematical Processes Algebraic Relationships	Algebraic Relationships Geometry	Algebraic Relationships Geometry
Task to be Accomplished	Task to be Accomplished	Task to be Accomplished
The cost of bringing in CCR for the concert is $20,000.00. How many tickets must be sold for $10.00 each to make a profit of $10,000.00 for Harbor House? How many tickets must be sold for $25.00 each? $30.00 each? $40.00 each? $50.00 each? $100.00 each? Compile your results in chart form. Brainstorm other fund-raising activities.	Develop a plan for seating in the gymnasium. Remember to leave room for a stage, aisles that meet fire codes, and exit paths. You will need to determine which chairs will be used, how many will fit, and diagram the gymnasium to scale so the maintenance staff can set up the gym for the concert. Work with the members of group 1 to develop an algebraic expression that can be used with varying ticket prices to determine how many tickets that must be sold.	With such a huge event taking place at CMS, parking may be a problem. What is the maximum number of vehicles that can be parked in the CMS and CES parking lots? What other areas could be used for parking? Develop a parking plan that will allow enough vehicles to be parked for the number of for the number of tickets that must be sold. You will have to talk to members of groups 1 and 2 to find out how many tickets need to be sold. Also, you will have to assume that each vehicle will have an average of 2 people in it. Coordinate the findings from all groups into a 10-minute proposal presentation. Discuss with those students working on seating how many chairs will fit in the gym and offer a recommendation for a ticket sale price.

Culminating Activity:
After all students have completed their tasks, they will meet as groups (all those working on the same task will meet together). A reporter from each group will be selected. The reporter will share the results of their task and explain the process that they followed to determine their answers.

Teacher Notes:
Evaluate and modify this lesson based on the success of the lesson and the performance of your students. (This would be a good place for your own reflection on the lesson.)

Appendix C
Guided Comprehension: Content Area Reading Strategies—Context Clues

Teacher-Directed Whole-Group Instruction (Day One)

Explain types of context clues using a PowerPoint.

Demonstrate how to use context clues by analyzing sentences found in teacher-selected texts.

Guide students to locate sentences in their reading material that use context clues.

Practice by exchanging the sentences found by students and analyzing the context clues.

Reflect on how and why context clues are important.

Comprehension Centers (Days 2, 3, 4)	**Small Group Instruction** (Days 2, 3, 4)	**Comprehension Routines** (Days 2, 3, 4)
1. Readers Handbook (pg. 615620) Take notes on each type of context clue.	**Group A:** Ukrainian Teen Life (Lexile 890)	Silent Reading Time While reading, complete self-selected vocabulary activity.
2. Bookmark Create a bookmark that summarizes each type of context clues.	**Group B:** Samoan Life (Lexile 990)	Use context clues to determine meanings of words and confirm with a dictionary.
3. Learning Chart (pg. 615620) Summarize information about context clues in chart-form. Practice writing sentences that use each type of clue.	**Group C:** South Korea (Lexile 1180) For each text, read together and silently. Locate and analyze context clues.	

Teacher-Facilitated Whole-Group Reflection and Goal Setting (Day 5)
1. Compare content of articles. What are the similarities and differences between the cultures represented?
2. Respond to the following prompt:
   How will context clues be helpful when reading a novel independently?
   How will context clues be helpful when reading a textbook independently?
   Evaluate your own ability to use context clues.
   What are your strengths and weaknesses?

Appendix D
Newsletter Creation

Create a Newsletter
Historical Society

Your Assignment:

Imagine that you are a member of a modern-day historical society devoted to studying a world empire. Create the monthly newsletter for your society.

Guidelines:

1. Your newsletter will contain information about the historical society and its area of interest.

2. The newsletter will include:

   ◆ A letter from the president of the society to its members

   ◆ An article about a famous person from your world empire

   ◆ An article about an important event in the history of your world empire

   ◆ An article about a cultural tradition important to your world empire

3. The newsletter must include ONE of the following:

   ◆ Additional news article

   ◆ Top 10 List

   ◆ Q &A

   ◆ Calendar of Events

   ◆ Contest sponsored by the society

3. The layout of the newsletter must include:

   ◆ Nameplate

   ◆ Graphics

   ◆ Reader Cues

   ◆ Effective Font Choices

Tips for Success

   ◆ Remember to write as though you actually are a member of a modern-day historical society. Be sure to create a name for your society and a persona for yourself.

   ◆ All historical information included in the newsletter should be accurate.

   ◆ Your audience is other members of the historical society.

Create a Newsletter
Family Times

Your Assignment:

Imagine that you are the father or mother of a family living in your assigned world empire at the height of its power. Create a newsletter that your family can send to their family members and friends depicting the important events in your family in the past year.

Guidelines:

1. Your newsletter will contain historically accurate information about the fictitious family you are a part of.
2. The newsletter will include:
   - A letter from the family to the readers of the newsletter
   - An article about a vacation your family went on during the year
   - An article about the family's views on an important figure or event
   - An article about a cultural tradition the family would have been part of
3. The newsletter must include ONE of the following:
   - An article about the jobs of the family members
   - An article describing where the family members live
   - A calendar of upcoming family events
   - Q &A
4. The layout of the newsletter must include:
   - Nameplate
   - Graphics
   - Reader Cues
   - Effective Font Choices

Tips for Success

- Remember to write as though you actually are part of a family living in your assigned world empire at the height of its power. Be sure to create a persona for yourself.
- All historical information included in the newsletter should be accurate.
- Your audience is your family and friends to whom the newsletter will be sent.

Create a Newsletter
Ancient Business Times

Your Assignment:

Imagine that you are the owner of a successful business in your assigned world empire at the height of its power. Create a newsletter that you can send to your customers.

Guidelines:

1. Your newsletter will contain information about your business and what it has to offer customers.
2. The newsletter will include:
- A letter from the owner to his/her customers
- An article about a new product or products you are featuring
- An article about a famous person that will be visiting your store
- An article about one of your employees
3. The newsletter must include TWO of the following:
- Additional article
- Top 10 List
- Q &A
- Calendar of Events
- Contest sponsored by the business
4. The layout of the newsletter must include:
- Nameplate
- Graphics
- Reader Cues
- Effective Font Choices

Tips for Success

- Remember to write as though you actually are a business owner living in your assigned world empire at the height of its power. Your business should be one that would actually have existed and flourished during the assigned time period. Be sure to create a persona for yourself.
- All historical information included in the newsletter should be accurate.
- Your audience is your customers to whom the newsletter will be sent.

Name _____ Block _____

Ideas, 15 points
Is it clear (no misunderstandings) and concise (main ideas stand out)?

_____ Contains all required written and graphic elements.
_____ Information is based on accurate historical research.
_____ Includes any background information necessary to understand information.

Organization, 20 points
Is it visually appealing?

_____ Grid (page layout) is effective
_____ Includes nameplate and graphics.
_____ Reader cues (bold, underline, font changes) are effective.
_____ Avoids common design problems.

Voice, 15 points
Is it informal and sincere?

_____ Professional, yet informal.
_____ Courteous and sincere at all times
_____ Successfully adopts the assigned persona

Word Choice, 10 points
Will the audience be able to read and understand the words?

_____ Writes words correctly and chooses the correct word for the situation.
_____ Attention to context (audience and purpose)

Sentence Fluency, 5 points
Is there variety in length and structure of sentences?

_____ Varied sentence structure and beginnings with transitions between ideas.

Conventions, 10 points
Is it completely error free?

_____ Final product is free of errors in spelling, grammar, punctuation, usage, and paragraphing.

Use of time, 5 points

_____ On-task during in-class work-time, project completed early or on-time.
_____ Engaged in peer revision and editing.
_____ out of 80 points possible

75 – 80	A	64	B-	55	D+
72 – 74	A-	62 – 63	C+	51 – 54	D
71	B+	59 – 61	C	48 – 50	D-
65 – 70	B	56 – 68	C-	0 – 47	F

Appendix E
Tiered Lesson

Teacher:	Betty Kovak
Grade Level:	8th Grade
Academic Area:	Reading
Lesson Title/Summary:	Making Word, Student-Designed Exercises

Students will work in groups to create Making Words-style exercises that emphasize word components and involve word play.

Standards Addressed:	A.12.1.1 C.12.3	
Lowest Performing Students	**Middle Performing Students**	**Highest Performing Students**
Hadda Badday (193, 191–200) Wishin Tohide (197, 201–210) Hardly Kare (214, 211–220)	Justin Themidle (228, 221–230) Even Kiel (228, 221–230) Aver Age (232, 221–230)	Excela Lot (235, 241–250) Sam Smart (233, (241–250) Bringit Ohn (246, 251–260)
NWEA Objective Strand	**NWEA Objective Strand**	**NWEA Objective Strand**
Word Analysis & Vocab Word Components	Word Analysis & Vocab Word Components Contextual Meaning & Vocab	Word Analysis & Vocab Word Components Contextual Meaning & Vocab
Task to be Accomplished	**Task to be Accomplished**	**Task to be Accomplished**
Write a Making Words lesson with five steps. The "big word" for the lesson will be: **performance**. For each step: • Include number of letters. • A sentence that uses the word. At least 3 of the steps must use a root, prefix, or suffix. Clearly indicate which steps these are.	Write a Making Words lesson with eight steps. The "big word" for the lesson will be: **deformity**. For each step: • Include number of letters. • A sentence that uses the word. At least 5 of the steps must use a root, prefix, or suffix. Clearly indicate which steps these are. Write a sentence that includes a context clue to define the "big word."	Write a Making Words lesson with 8 steps. The "big word" for the lesson must use the root word "form" and have at least 8 letters. For each step: Include number of letters. A sentence that uses the word. At least 8 of the steps must use a root, prefix, or suffix. Clearly indicate which steps these are. Write a sentence that includes a context clue to define the "big word."

Culminating Activity:
Each group will "teach" their lesson to the large group. All students will be exposed to roots, prefixes, and suffixes in each exercise and will discuss context clues.

Teacher Notes:

Bibliography

American Association of School Administrators. (2002). *Using data to improve schools: What's working?* Arlington, VA: Author. Retrieved November 5, 2006, from http://www.aasa.org/cas/usingdatatoimproveschools.pdf.

Amrein, A. L., & Berliner, D. C. (2002, March 28). High-stakes testing, uncertainty, and student learning. *Educational Policy Analysis Archives, 10*(18). Retrieved November 5, 2003 from http://epaa.asu.edu/epaa/v10n18/.

Anderson, G. L., Herr, K., & Nihlen, A. S. (1994). *Studying your own school: An educator's guide to qualitative practitioner research.* Thousands Oaks, CA: Corwin Press.

Bernhardt, V. L. (2000). New routes open when one type of data crosses another. *Journal of Staff Development, 21*(1), 1–6.

Bernhardt, V. L. (2004). *Data analysis for continuous schoolwide improvement* (2nd ed.). Larchmont, NY: Eye On Education.

Black, P. (1998). Inside the black box: Raising standards through classroom assessment. *Phi Delta Kappan, 80*(2), 139–149.

Black, P., & Wiliam, D. (1998). Assessment and classroom learning. *Assessment in Education, 5*(1), 7–74.

Blink, R. (2005). *How do K–12 school districts build data-driven systems and utilize those systems to improve student achievement?* Unpublished doctoral dissertation, University of Wisconsin–Madison.

Bogan, R. C., & Biklen, S. K. (1998). *Qualitative research for education: An introduction to theory and methods.* Needham Heights, MA: Allyn & Bacon.

Clegg, S. R., Hardy, C., and Nord, W. R. (1996). *Handbook of organization studies.* Thousand Oaks, CA: Sage.

Coyle, J. (2001). Final answer? Computer testing's real payoff, this district found, is fast and flexible data. *Electronic School*, March. Retrieved November 5, 2006, from http://www.electronic-school.com/2001/03/0301f8.html.

Creswell, J. W. (1994). *Research design: Qualitative and quantitative approaches.* Thousand Oaks, CA: Sage.

Cromley, A. (2000). *Using student assessment data: What can we learn from schools?* (NCREL Policy Issues No. 6). Washington, DC: North Central Regional Educational Laboratory.

Datnow, A., & Springfield, S. (2000). Working together for reliable school reform. *Journal of Education for Students Placed at Risk, 5* (1–2), 183–201.

Deming, W. E. (2000). *Out of the crisis.* Cambridge, MA: MIT Press.

Downey, C. J., English, F. W., Frase, L. E., Melton, R. G., Poston, W. K., & Steffy, B. E. (2002). *50 ways to raise students' test scores: Standards for high performing schools; Leveling the playing field for all learners.* Johnston, IA: Curriculum Management Systems.

English, F. W. (2000). *Deciding what to teach and test* (Millennium ed.). Thousand Oaks, CA: Corwin Press.

Hallinger, P., & Heck, R. H. (1996). Reassessing the principal's role in school effectiveness: A review of empirical research, 1980–1995. *Educational Administration Quarterly 32*(1), 5–44.

Haney, W. (2000, August 19). The myth of the Texas miracle in education. *Education Policy Analysis Archives, 8*(41). Retrieved November 5, 2006, from http://epaa.asu.edu/epaa/v8n41.

Hittleman, D. R., & Simon, A. J. (1992). *Interpreting educational research: An introduction for consumers of research* New York: Macmillan.

Hoy, W. K., & Miskel, C. G. (1982). *Educational administration: Theory, research, and practice* (2nd ed.). New York: Random House.

Kohn, A. (2000). *The case against standardized testing: Raising the scores, ruining the schools.* Portsmouth, NH: Heinemann.

Liddle, K. (2000). Data-driven success: how one elementary school mined assessment data to improve instruction. *Electronic School,* March. Retrieved November 5, 2006, from www.electronic-school.com/2000/03/0300f3.html.

Linn, R. (1998). *Assessments and accountability* (Technical Rep. No. 490). Boulder: Center for the Study of Evaluation, University of Colorado at Boulder.

Marzano, R. J. (2000). *Transforming classroom grading.* Alexandria, VA: Association for Supervision and Curriculum Development.

Marzano, R. J., Pickering, D. J., & Pollock, J. E. (2001). *Classroom instruction that works: Research-based strategies for increasing student achievement.* Alexandria, VA: Association for Supervision and Curriculum Development.

Middlewood, D., Coleman, M., & Lumby, J. (1999). *Practitioner research in education: Making a difference.* Thousand Oaks, CA: Sage.

Newmann, F. M., King, B., & Youngs, P. (2000, April). *Professional development that addresses school capacity.* Paper presented at the Annual Meeting of the American Educational Research Association, New Orleans, LA.

Northwest Evaluation Association. (2001). *Administration professional learning guide.* Portland, OR: Author.

Ohanian, S. (1999). *One size fits few: The folly of educational standards.* Portsmouth, NH: Heinemann.

Older students need reading support, too. (February 2005). *Reading Today,* 22(4), 11.

Pascopella, A. (2003). *District administration: The next challenge.* Norwalk, CT: Professional Media Group.

Patton, M. L. (2001). *Questionnaire research: A practical guide.* Los Angeles: Pyrczak.

Perrone, V. (1991a). *Expanding student assessment.* Alexandria, VA: Association for Supervision and Curriculum Development.

Perrone, V. (1991b). *On standardized testing* (ERIC Digest No. ED338445). Urbana, IL: ERIC Clearinghouse on Elementary and Early Childhood Education.

Popham, J. W. (2001). *The truth about testing.* Alexandria, VA: Association for Supervision and Curriculum Development.

Sagor, R. (2000). *Guiding school improvement with action research.* Alexandria, VA: Association for Supervision and Curriculum Development.

Sargent, J. K. (2006). CESA 7 School Improvement Services. Data retreat workshop and materials http://www.cesa7.k12.wi.us/newweb/content/schoolimprove/Data-Retreats/

Schmoker, M. (1999). *Results: The key to continuous school improvement* (2nd ed.). Alexandria, VA: Association for Supervision and Curriculum Development.

Scholtes, P. (1994). *The team handbook for educators.* Madison, WI: Joiner Associates.

Senge, P. (1994). *The fifth discipline: The art and practice of the learning organization.* New York: Doubleday.

Shafritz, J. M., & Ott, J. S. (1987). *Classics of organization theory* (2nd ed.). Chicago: Dorsey Press.

Stiggins, R. J., Arter, J. A., Chappuis, J., & Chappuis, S. (2004). *Classroom assessment for student learning: Doing it right, using it well.* Portland, OR: Assessment Training Institute.

Streifer, P. A. (2002). *Using data to make better educational decisions.* Lanham, MD: Scarecrow Press.

Stronge, J. H. (2002). *Qualities of effective teachers.* Alexandria, VA: Association for Supervision and Curriculum Development.

Tomlinson, C. A. (1999). *The differentiated classroom: Responding to the needs of all learners.* Alexandria, VA: Association for Supervision and Curriculum Development.

Youngs, P., & King, M. B. (2002). Principal leadership for professional development to build school capacity. *Educational Administration Quarterly* 38(5), 643–670.